"Dear Doctor Piano..."

Piano Facts and Fun by Ken Burton

Published by Dot Press

"Dear Doctor Piano..."

First Canadian Edition
ISBN: 1-895510-06-6

Published by Dot Press
1 Willow Cres. S.W.
Calgary, Alberta T3C 3B8

Illustrations by Ben Crane, Spur Graphics
Sundre, Alberta, Canada

Design by Epix Design Inc,
Calgary, Alberta, Canada

Printed in Canada

953213

INTRODUCTION:

Here's a book of facts and fun about pianos–questions and answers to help you better understand your piano. My hope is that with increased appreciation of this marvelous instrument you will also learn how to care for it more effectively. Thus, your piano will become a more beautiful and satisfying part of your life.

Because these letters are answers to people's questions, some overlapping of ideas occurs. This is done purposefully so that important concepts can be expanded and reinforced.

I have used laymen's language in my answers, some humor and enough simplicity that young piano pupils will be able to understand and enjoy them.

Of course, it will be obvious to you that the tuning and repair prices quoted do not apply everywhere. They are valid only in Calgary, Alberta in 1993 and even there they will vary from one technician to another.

Please don't be misled by the fact that I refer to the piano technician as "he". This is to avoid the awkwardness of "he/she" and "him/her". In actual fact, many women have entered the piano service profession in recent years. The same policy applies to piano teachers. Both sexes share these important occupations.

In the section on "The Weather And Your Piano", the facts of climate and humidity fluctuations are based on conditions found on the Canadian Prairies where summer rains create a moderate indoor humidity but cold winters (and the heating required) cause the air to become excessively dry. If you live in California or New England or some other region where the climate is markedly different from this, call your favorite tuner and ask him to explain both the yearly humidity changes and the tuning schedules made necessary by them.

My thanks go to all the curious people who asked me these questions and made this book possible. Love and appreciation go to my wife, Dot, who patiently put up with a guy who was there but "wasn't", during the writing process. A big thank you also goes to Mike Swendsen and Don Rose, Registered Technicians of the Piano Technicians Guild, for their suggestions. Thanks, too, to Ron Giesbrecht and John Wright; also Kent Webb. But my greatest thanks goes to the Heavenly Father who gives me daily guidance and comfort through His Son, Jesus Christ.

Doctor Piano

a.k.a. Ken Burton

403-242-0799

TABLE OF CONTENTS

BOY

DOG

TUNING THE PIANO

MOM

CARING FOR YOUR PIANO

SALESMAN

THE WEATHER AND YOUR PIANO

THE PIANO TUNER

TEACHER

DR. PIANO

Buying a Piano...

Dear Doctor Piano,

We need to get a piano for our children. How do we go about choosing the right piano to buy? I'm scared we'll make a mistake.

Doreen B.

Dear Doreen,

Your fears are well founded. Lots of people make mistakes and find themselves stuck with poorly made instruments which are not giving satisfaction.

Buying a new piano is a tricky business. Every salesman, every piano teacher and every piano tuner has a favorite make to recommend and many of them are terrible. I, too, have strong feelings about certain makes of pianos but not all tuners agree with me.

Here are three common sense principles:

1. Buy the most expensive piano you can afford. Saving money by buying cheaper musical instruments usually produces dissatisfaction.

2. Buy a piano made by a reputable company, one which has a good production volume, and offers a manufacturer-backed warranty.

3. Buy a piano favored by most music institutions (conservatories and universities). They know by experience which are the best, most trouble-free pianos.

It's important, Doreen, to determine in advance what kind of piano sound you like: mellow, brilliant, loud, soft. Then, when you go shopping, take a pianist with you and ask for his feelings about each piano he plays. Listen to low, middle and high notes. And don't forget to try out several pianos of each brand and model. Often, depending on the make and price range, there are surprising individual differences and you want to find the one that exactly suits you.

Buying a used piano is even trickier. You could be buying someone else's problems and there's usually no warranty to bail you out if you get a lemon. But, if you see one you like, above all, call your favorite tuner and have him evaluate it for you. He'll be able to warn you of problems and advise you if this is a piano that can meet your needs.

Happy hunting, Doreen.

Doctor Piano

Dear Doctor Piano,

Can you help me to know which new piano to buy? I'm confused because every salesman seems to contradict the others.

Nickie

Dear Nickie,

This is the question I'm asked more than any other. It really is a perplexing problem. Let me compare it to buying a new car because this is a more familiar process.

Some pianos are like Volkswagen cars, some like Toyotas, others like Fords and Chevs. Some are like Buicks, Lincolns and Cadillacs. A few are like Mercedez-Benzes and Rolls Royces. You know which are which: price makes the difference (with a few exceptions due to the economies of the manufacturing countries).

The point is, Nickie, they'll all get you from point A to point B. It's just that some will do it with more style and beauty and class. That's something you have to decide–how much beauty do you want to purchase?(beauty of sound as well as beauty of appearance) No matter what the salesman tells you, a Jeep is not as beautiful as a Lambhorgini.

Some are more sturdy than others, some cost more to operate than others, some will keep their beauty longer than others.

What we all want to watch out for is: some of them are "lemons". And you can't find this out from the salesman. He makes it sound like a "Dream Boat". You have to ask a mechanic (Piano Technician). I guess that's why I get so many calls on this subject.

Check out your local library. You'll find books that'll explain some of the mysteries of pianos and will give you valuable pointers on choosing a good instrument.

Keep looking, Nickie, you'll find one.

Doctor Piano

Dear Doctor Piano,

When I go into a piano store, I'm really confused. The pianos all look the same but some are thousands of dollars more than others. What's the difference between a high-priced and a low-priced piano?

Jim and Shirley D.

Dear Jim and Shirley,

Yes, it's baffling. Actually, telling the difference between a high-priced and low-priced piano is not the real problem. It's easy to tell a poor piano from a good one. Poorer materials are used. Construction parts are thinner and more flimsy. The finish may be second rate and the tone obviously weak and full of false sounds. There'll be noticeable flaws in workmanship. Not hard to tell them apart.

The real problem is trying to make the comparison between a medium quality piano and a really good one. The materials used may be exactly the same. Both may be beautifully finished. In fact, the medium piano may have a more elegant exterior and finish. If you look at the inside, they appear identical.

In spite of all these similarities, there may be $1000 to $2000 difference in price. Why?

The answer is workmanship and tone. In ways that you can't see, the craftsmanship of the better piano is more precise and perfect. Extra pains have been taken to ensure that every dimension, every movement, every resonating point is exactly right. If you could watch the process, it would remind you of a dedicated craftsman building a fine violin. The result is a superior tone in the piano and this is what you are willing to pay for.

Now comes another problem: When you play a piano in one store and another piano in a different store, it's almost impossible to remember the tone and compare them in your mind. Differences in the rooms where the pianos are sitting also affect the tone greatly. Your favorite piano tuner can be a big help to you. He's used to listening to the sound of different pianos in different environments and he can help to identify tonal qualities for you.

I know there are lots of people who can't tell the difference between a piano with average tone and one with superior tone, but when you hear a performance on the better one, you smile and say, "That's special".

Doctor Piano

As we think about bringing a piano into our home, we're wondering about the differences between an upright piano and a grand piano. Would it be better for us to have an upright or a grand?

Neil M.

Dear Neil,

Lots of things need to be considered here, aside from the floor space required and the price.

You may have heard the name: "Upright Grand". Take it from me: "There's no such animal". An upright is an upright and a grand is a grand. Some piano manufacturers invented that name for advertising purposes and applied it to certain upright pianos because they were of high quality or they had some features that imitated those of a grand piano.

An upright is an upright because the strings stand upright (or vertical) and a grand is a grand because the strings lie horizontal. However, there are lots of other differences. Without getting too technical, let me make these comparisons:

Grand pianos sound clearer and more resonant because the "kidney" shape of the piano allows string sizes to match more efficiently to soundboard area. Their actions are more responsive because the mechanism is more sophisticated. The bass notes have a "truer" quality because the strings are made longer and thinner.

For all the same reasons, upright pianos usually sound poorer than grands. But there are exceptions. There are some tall uprights being made today which are equal or superior to a small grand. But they also cost just about as much money.

So, there are a lot of questions to be asked in choosing a piano: Which is more important—appearance or sound? Do you want a tiny piano that will hide in a corner? (You may have to put up with a poor action and sound.) Do you want a large upright to highlight a living room wall and give great music? (Expect to spend a sizeable amount of money). Do you want an instrument that will make your child feel like a concert pianist every time he sits down to practise? (Then, buy a good grand piano, the largest you can fit into the space and the budget you have available.)

Choose well: "A thing of beauty is a joy forever."

Doctor Piano

Dear Doctor Piano,

I was amazed when I went into a piano store the other day. There were so many different models and prices and sizes. Why do they have so many different pianos?

Margaret C.

Dear Margaret,

I guess there are so many sizes of pianos because people are different and they all want different things. Some want a wee little piano they can hide in a corner, others want an average size piano with a luxurious furniture style and others want a big, black piano that sounds like an instrument for the concert hall. So – manufacturers make them that way.

Each size of acoustic piano has its advantages and drawbacks.

The smallest upright is about 36 inches tall and 55 inches wide. It's a cute little thing but its small size also gives out a very small sound. It may lack some of the notes and strings of a normal piano. It's okay for casual use though a serious piano pupil would find it unsatisfactory.

The next size is about 42 inches tall and 57 inches wide. It has a full keyboard and usually features a variety of furniture styles: American, Mediterranean Spanish, French Provincial, European, etc. It's a nice piece of furniture and a very worthwhile musical instrument, certainly adequate for a piano pupil. But an advanced music student may want something larger.

Next in line comes the 45-inch size. Often it has a plainer style because it is not primarily a piece of furniture. It has longer strings and a bigger soundboard for a larger, more resonant tone. This is a good size for piano teachers and school use.

Above this comes the 48-inch size, sometimes called the Conservatory model. Extra care and workmanship go into this piano to make it especially responsive and resonant. It can provide the resources of touch and tone which will challenge the high level performer.

There's still one more model, the 52-inch size. This piano is designed to compete with small grand pianos. You wouldn't want to place it in a little room in your home because its volume might drive you right out. It'll equal a small grand in responsiveness and tone, but it may equal it in price, too.

Lots of choices to suit lots of people, Margaret.

Doctor Piano

Dear Doctor Piano,

We've been shopping for a piano for our family and we noticed that every salesman tells us how wonderful his piano is. He gives a long list of advantages for his product but we worry about what he is not telling us. Can we really trust the piano salesman?

Jack and Phyl W.

Dear Jack and Phyl,

It depends. He tells you a lot of stuff about spruce soundboards and laminated pinblocks. You must realize that he'll use any talking point he can think of to convince you that you should buy his piano instead of someone else's.

A rule of thumb to follow is: you get what you pay for. In purchasing a new musical instrument, there are seldom any bargains. Manufacturing an instrument which has a beautiful sound and rich resonance, is an expensive, time-consuming process. If you try to save money, you may wind up with a piano that was put together by assembly line workers instead of the highly skilled piano craftsmen who know how to bring out the tone.

But, when you've decided which name-brand piano to buy, the salesman can be helpful. Describe the kind of music you'll be playing and ask him which size and model will suit your needs. Then tell him about the room the piano will be in: the size, the drapes and rugs, and whether you like the piano to sound brilliant or mellow. A knowledgable salesman knows the tone of his pianos and he'll give you good advice.

After all this, if you're still not sure, tell the salesman that you want the piano in your home on a trial basis. It'll sound vastly different in your home than it did in the store and you want to be sure that you are really pleased with it.

Of course, your piano tuner's advice will help, too. He's used to listening to piano tone from a variety of different makes of pianos in a variety of different settings and he'll be glad to share his knowledge with you.

Doctor Piano

Dear Doctor Piano,

I've been taking my little boy with me to look for a piano to buy. He's small for his age and many of the pianos seem too big for him. Either the bench is too tall or the keyboard is too high. Isn't there a standard height for a piano bench?

Doug H.

Dear Doug,

It's difficult, isn't it? You want the piano and bench to fit him now while he's small and still fit him later when he grows taller.

Unfortunately, there's no uniform standard height for piano benches and neither is there a uniform standard for keyboard height. But perhaps that's just as well because people are all different, aren't they?

However, the critical measurement is the difference between the bench and the keyboard. It usually varies between 8 1/2 and 10 1/2 inches.

The problem, of course, comes when the bench and piano that you've purchased, don't fit your child. The telephone book may help but what if the bench is already too high? Do you saw some off the legs?

The best answer, Doug, is an adjustable chair or bench. They sell for $200 to $800 and the good ones will last a lifetime. If you have one, you can adjust it to the exact needs of your growing child – the optimum height.

The next question is, "How do you know when the height is right?" Here's how to tell: Have your child sit erect on the bench with wrists straight, fingers curved and resting on the keys. Adjust the height of the bench until the child's forearm is level with the floor. That's it!

Ask your teacher if she feels the use of an adjustable foot rest and pedal extensions would help your small person to play a large piano more easily.

When the bench is at the proper height and his feet are resting on the floor or on a low stool, your child will be comfortable, properly balanced and poised to play his best music.

Doctor Piano

Dear Doctor Piano,

When I've been in the piano stores lately, I've noticed that they have electronic pianos for sale. They sure are small. Are they any good?

Kelly C.

Dear Kelly,

O yes, many of them are very good.

But, what I think you're asking, Kelly, is, "Should I buy an electronic piano instead of a *real* piano?" As always, the answer is, "It depends." It depends what you expect from a piano.

If you want a small, lightweight keyboard instrument for casual playing, with a fairly accurate piano sound (except for the inescapable "loudspeaker" quality), a good electronic piano may please you. You'll also have the advantage of being able to play a variety of other sounds on the same instrument (organ, synthesizer, etc.)

But, be prepared for high depreciation costs as compared to a traditional acoustic piano. Electronic instruments soon go out of date as new models are introduced. It won't have the touch of a standard piano, either, only a simulation. And it won't stand up as well as a good piano mechanism to the thousands of hours of daily practice which a developing pianist needs over the years. Another thing you'll miss is the changing tone quality which should accompany loud and soft playing unless you spend a lot more.

On the other hand, if you want the feel and sound of a true piano (no loudspeakers), an instrument which will keep its value or even appreciate, one that will provide daily practicing for 50 to 75 years, a beautiful piece of furniture that will enhance your home – then purchase a good acoustic piano.

Do I sound prejudiced, Kelly? Probably. I guess I am. I guess, for me, nothing can take the place of the wood and felt and steel that I've worked with for so many years.

Will electronic pianos ever "take over" the field? *Never!*

Electric guitars didn't, did they?

Doctor Piano

Dear Doctor Piano,

We finally got a piano and found a piano teacher for our son Bruce but he doesn't seem to spend very long at the piano. How can I get him to practice his piano lessons?

Gordon M.

Dear Gordon,

To tell you the truth, that's out of my line. I'm qualified to make the piano work, not the pupil.

You may have to resort to all kinds of encouragements, coaxing and bribes. But eventually, no matter what you try, young people have to come to the place where they practice because of the beauty of the music and the beauty of the musical instrument.

Too many beginning piano pupils have to practice on a piano that has no beauty in it. The sound is plunky, the action is uneven and the tuning is jangly. It's no wonder that most of them never discover the beauty of piano music. If your piano is like that, Gordon, your coaxing may fall on deaf ears. Your child may feel it's like trying to learn to ride on a bicycle that has flat tires.

Call your favorite tuner and tell him that you want your piano to be put into the condition that will provide the greatest possible encouragement for your child to practice.

Then, call your piano teacher. Tell her what you've done and ask her for some more suggestions.

I hope this helps, Gordon.

Doctor Piano

Dear Doctor Piano,

You mentioned to me that you feel I should trade my piano for a better one. Why can't I just keep the same piano always?

Lena S.

Dear Lena,

You don't expect to do that with other musical instruments or with your automobile, so why the piano?

A young lady told me the other day, with pride, "My mother got her music degree on this piano and so did I."

That's alright, except that it was a little piano with a mediocre action and a plunky sound. I thought, What a shame! Playing such high level music on such a poor piano is like trying to play baseball with a plastic bat.

You wouldn't do that to your child if he or she were taking violin lessons, Lena. You'd get a very average violin to start with, and then, if he showed interest and talent, you'd get him a better violin, one which would have the tonal resources to challenge and excite him to achieve beauty in his playing. It might cost you $5000 or more.

And then—when it looked like music would become an important part of his life—you'd help him get a really good one, one that can sing like the angels in heaven. It might cost more than your house.

Why not do the same with pianos? Start with a less expensive one, perhaps a good used piano which you can get for $2000 or less. Then, if your child shows promise (ask your piano teacher) trade up at the end of two or three years. Your favorite tuner will help you to identify an instrument that will give your child the best possible encouragement to develop as a musician.

Doctor Piano

Dear Doctor Piano,

We finally did it! We bought the piano we've been wanting for so long. Now I realize how little I know about it. What should I expect of the new piano they delivered to our home?

Jan G.

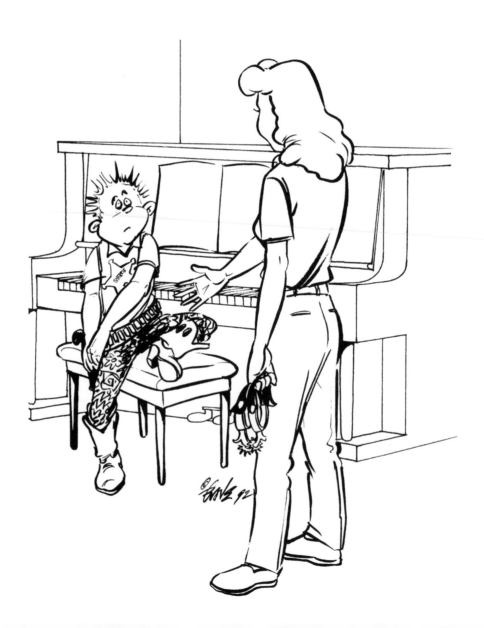

Dear Jan,

Good question! But, I don't think you're asking about the piano's materials and workmanship. Problems in this area will be covered by the warranty (make sure it has a *manufacturer-backed* warranty.) I think you're asking about the way your piano should work and sound when it's brand new.

Don't worry about the piano being in or out of tune. New pianos go out of tune quickly during the first two years. Anyway, dealers usually arrange for a free tuning after it's been in your home for a couple of months–long enough for it to get adjusted to the new humidity conditions.

It goes without saying that the piano should perform without squeaks or clicks or sticking keys. Call your dealer and he'll make sure these obvious problems are corrected without any cost to you.

However, there are other concerns which are not so obvious. You, as the purchaser, have the right to expect the piano to be at standard pitch with its action properly regulated and voiced. If not, you'll have to pay for these corrections at some later time. When the piano tuner comes to give the piano its first tuning in your home, ask him to make sure these standards have been met.

But now, my friend, there's another side to the coin. Your piano dealer has rights, too. His reputation depends on how well your piano works and sounds. If you neglect the tuning and the thing sounds as sour as green lemons, you're not playing fair. The dealer who sold you the piano has the right to expect you to arrange to have it tuned and serviced properly.

A new piano takes extra tuning: three or four times the first year, two times the second year and regularly after that. It'll cost you something, but it's worth it. If the piano plays like a dream and sounds like a string of pearls, everybody will be happy–you, your family, your piano teacher, your dealer and the piano tuner.

Right?...Right!

Doctor Piano

Dear Doctor Piano,

We are enjoying our new piano very much and it seems flawless. But we got thinking: what if some defect shows up? What kind of a warranty do you get with a new piano?

Tony D.

Dear Tony,

This is a complicated question to answer but a very important one, so I'll try to keep my answer short. When you're buying a piano you need to know what protection you're getting for your investment. Pianos can develop problems costing thousands of dollars to repair, so you need some kind of guarantee.

Most pianos come with a warranty against defects in materials and workmanship for a 10-year period. Since problems usually show up in the first five to ten years of a piano's life, this is adequate. But don't expect it to include tuning, normal wear or damage caused by exposure to moisture, severe dryness or extreme heat and cold.

Because the warranty is only as good as the organization behind it, make sure it's backed by the manufacturer, not just the dealer or distributor.

There are two kinds of warranties: *Full* and *Limited.*

A *full* warranty covers both parts and labor and the cost of shipping the piano to a repair depot. It's often transferable to new owners of the piano and includes an obligation to provide a replacement unit or a full refund if a repair isn't possible. This warranty isn't voided by a failure to send in the warranty card or by using a piano technician other than the one provided by the dealer.

A *limited* warranty may cover the cost of parts only (usually a tiny fraction of the total bill). It may cover only the original purchaser and it may not cover the cost of sending the piano to the factory if that becomes necessary.

Tony, you need to find out what kind of warranty you're getting. Find the warranty card and keep it with your important papers. Well made pianos seldom give any trouble, but if it happens, you don't want any expensive surprises.

Doctor Piano

Dear Doctor Piano,

They brought our new piano yesterday. It looks so shiny and sounds so wonderful. We want it to stay like that as long as possible. They told us how to clean the finish but what about the rest of it? How should we care for our new piano?

Edna B.

Dear Edna,

Good for you. You realize that new pianos have special needs.

Some people think, "It's new. It should be good for ten years without touching it." Quite the contrary. New pianos should be checked three or four times the first year and twice the second year.

Seems strange, doesn't it? It's because all the parts of the piano are new. The strings will stretch more at first (ever put new strings on a guitar?) The soundboard will settle, causing the piano to go out of tune. And things are happening in other parts of the piano, too. Wooden pieces are shrinking slightly, felt bushings and pads are compressing. This causes changes in the adjustments of the action.

Call your favorite tuner every six months. He'll check the piano for these changes and tune it each time. Then, at the end of the two-year period, ask him to give it a thorough check-up to see if the screws need tightening or the action needs adjusting.

What then? Your piano will be in first class condition and, with regular tuning, will give great satisfaction to you and your family for many years to come.

Doctor Piano

Dear Doctor Piano,

We bought our new piano six months ago. Today, the tuner phoned to say it should be tuned again. It sounds fine to me. What should I do?

Dale S.

Dear Dale,

Check with the store where you purchased the piano. They usually recommend a maintenance program which includes three or four tunings the first year, two tunings the second year and one or two tunings per year for the rest of the piano's life.

"But it's brand new!" you say.

I know, Dale, and that's the point. It's like buying a new car. During the "break-in" period, the dealer recommends oil changes at frequent intervals. If you value your car, you don't skip these just because it runs fine. Changing the oil only once a year would be neglectful.

It's the same with a new piano. It has a "break-in" period, too. The new strings stretch, the new wood shrinks and the new felts settle. Tuning it only once a year would be neglectful. When the tuner finally comes, he has to raise the pitch an extreme amount–which can damage parts of your new piano.

Your brand new piano will sound better and last longer if you follow the program of servicing recommended by the dealer.

Doctor Piano

Dear Doctor Piano,

We recently got a new piano and it has a polished ebony finish. It's so beautiful – like a mirror. Can you help me keep it looking like this?

Chris G.

Dear Chris,

Have no fear. The new furniture finishes are a lot like new-born babies – they're tougher than you think. However, there are some do's and don'ts.

There are two basic types of piano finishes and each should be treated differently. The old familiar one is varnish but more recently, many pianos are now beautifully finished with lacquer or polyester resin.

For the old finishes, you should use a light polish / cleaner combination (without wax or silicone because these build up and cause trouble.) One refinisher recommends a mixture of lemon oil and vinegar.

However, the new polyester or lacquer finishes are a whole different ballgame – even easier to look after. To keep them looking beautiful, clean with a soft cloth dampened with water and polish with a dry one (cloth diapers are ideal). To get rid of finger prints, use the same procedure but add a little elbow grease.

Warning: Use nothing but water or a product recommended by your piano dealer. Many cleansers are very harmful to pianos and if you should happen to get ahold of the wrong one, you could be faced with a big repair bill.

It goes without saying that you should never place a drinking glass or cup on a piano or any piece of furniture that you value. Coasters are cheap. Have lots of them handy. And potted plants are dynamite. *Never! Never! Never!*

But if, after some years, your piano begins to suffer from cloudiness of the finish or scratches and chips, you need the skills of a professional refinisher. (Ask your favorite tuner to recommend one.) Scratches and chips cost about $35.00 or more to repair. A light refinish spray is available for $300 plus the cost of taking the piano to the refinisher's shop and back. The cloudiness and scuffs will be gone and your piano will look new again.

Follow these instructions, Chris, and the finish on your piano will probably last longer than you do.

Doctor Piano

Dear Doctor Piano,

We need to get a piano so our children can take lessons, but the new ones are so much money. You never know if the kids will really be interested. Is it possible to buy a good used piano?

Nick T.

Dear Nick,

Yes, it certainly is, but there are pluses and minuses in the process.

On the plus side: a piano is designed to last for many years, so it's possible to buy one that has lots of life left in it. And, in some cases, buying an older piano will get you the kind of careful workmanship you seldom find these days. (A new Volkswagon isn't better than a used Rolls Royce.) And, of course, you expect to save money by buying a used piano.

The minus side: the warranty may have run out or may be non-transferable. And, it's hard to tell what the piano has been through, perhaps damaging heat conditions or excessive moisture or dryness. You may be buying someone else's troubles. In some cases, the piano may be worn out. Either you have to spend a lot of money on it or else, throw it out.

At this point, Nick, the piano/automobile analogy breaks down. A worn out car simply refuses to run. But a worn out piano keeps clunking along, frustrating and discouraging children who are trying to learn music.

Your piano dealer may have some used pianos for sale and may offer a limited guarantee on their condition. You'll also notice pianos for sale in the classified ads of your local newspaper. But– *buyer beware!* It's a jungle out there. There are some beauties but there are also some lemons. And, to borrow a phrase from the beauty industry, "Only your tuner knows for sure."

Call your favorite piano tuner. He'll help you to know which piano to steer clear of and which one to go for–and how much to pay. Remember to give him something for his time and expertise–he's saving you a lot of money and grief.

Doctor Piano

Dear Doctor Piano,

I don't know if my little Johnny is musical or not and I hate to invest a lot of money in a nice piano in case he doesn't take to it. Is it possible to rent one for a while to see what happens?

Mike S.

Dear Mike,

Yes, it's possible but for a couple of reasons, it may not be a good idea.

Very few dealers offer a straight rental contract on a piano. Usually, it's a rental-purchase arrangement. You rent the piano for six months at $50 - $150 per month (Grands start around $125.) Then, you have to choose whether to continue to rent or purchase the instrument. If you decide to keep it, the first six months rent you've paid is deducted from the purchase price.

So far so good. But the catch is: the purchase price you end up with is the full list price—no discounts, no sale prices, no bargaining. So, you might wind up paying $1000 too much for your piano. However, in spite of all this, you may feel it's better than buying a piano and having to sell it again if Johnny doesn't respond. (You might lose more than that in depreciation.)

But there's another catch—a much more serious one. Your primary purpose in having the piano is so that Johnny will learn to play and enjoy it for years to come—right? Well, this six-month plan may backfire. It's far too short a time to decide his musical future. And, to make things worse, a short-term financial commitment may produce a short-term musical commitment in Johnny's mind. You definitely don't want that.

The deeper your family involvement in piano music, the more likely that Johnny will continue to study and enjoy it. If you play the piano or play records of good piano music, if you keep him company while he practices, if you go with him to lessons and recitals, if you make the piano a permanent, vital part of your home—chances are a lot better that he'll stick with it. No guarantees, just a better hope.

Tough decision to make, isn't it, Mike? Good luck.

Doctor Piano

Dear Doctor Piano,

It's a crying shame the poor pianos that some children have to practice on. Why do parents make their children start lessons on such terrible old pianos?

It's just like sending a child out to learn how to ice-skate with a broken-down old pair of skates that bend over at the ankles. No caring parent would do that. Yet, they buy a big, old piano for $800 that has such a booming sound and such a worn out action that the poor child can't begin to control it, let alone learn to produce the subtleties of tone that make a pianist.

What can we do to make sure that children have high quality pianos to practice on?

Irate Piano Teacher

Dear Irate Teacher,

You have certainly identified an urgent problem. Here are some suggestions that may help:

1. Parents planning to start their children in piano lessons should select a teacher before choosing a piano. If you don't know of one in your area, call the Registered Music Teachers' Association. They'll give you a list of teachers and tell you which ones enjoy teaching beginners.

2. When planning to buy a piano, parents should get the advice and help of their piano teacher to make sure the child has an instrument capable of supporting the technique she'll be teaching. If you wish to purchase a used instrument, *be sure* to have it examined by a piano tuner to avoid costly disappointments.

3. Often, a "boomy" old piano with a sloppy action can be adjusted and softened by the piano technician so that it can meet your standards of touch and tone.

Thank you for your letter. I can tell that you have the welfare of your pupils at heart.

Doctor Piano

Dear Doctor Piano,

We want our children to start piano lessons this fall but we don't have a piano. My brother-in-law has an old one that he'll let us have. It's not much of a piano but it'll do for a starter. Is that alright?

Richard R.

Dear Richard,

No, it's not right at all, and it may be the reason why many children quit piano lessons so soon.

Some of the things that are out of kilter with poor pianos can cause real discouragement to beginning musicians. The piano may go out of tune quickly. The sound may be either too muffled or too harsh. The touch may be too heavy for little fingers or so loose that proper control is impossible. Some notes may refuse to play. Others may keep on ringing after the key is released. The piano may be tuned below standard pitch, making proper ear training impossible.

If these conditions exist, Richard, your child will look in vain for beauty in piano sound to encourage his efforts. Instead, he'll experience disappointment and frustration which may be enough to end his piano playing career forever.

So if you want your child to begin lessons on a used piano, call your favorite tuner and ask him to evaluate the piano to see if it can be brought into good playing condition – including both tuning and action efficiency. Then, ask your piano teacher to check it out to see if it meets the standards demanded by her teaching techniques.

It sounds like a lot of trouble and expense, doesn't it? But, if you do it, you may save your child's musical career.

Doctor Piano

Dear Doctor Piano,

My piano doesn't get played anymore and I think I'd like to sell it so someone else can get some use out of it. How can I find out how much it's worth?

Willa S.

Dear Willa,

Ask your favorite tuner. Pay him to come to your home and thoroughly inspect the piano.

He'll be looking for loose tuning pins (seriously reduces the value), split bass bridge (repair is necessary), worn hammers (an easier repair), loose action parts (time consuming to fix) and the condition of the cabinet (refinishing is expensive).

He'll also want to note the brand name. Some makes of pianos are of such high quality that even if some of the above defects exist, the piano is still very valuable.

Based on all of this information (it's a good idea to get it in writing), your tuner will give you a ball park figure for a selling price. *Caution:* don't sell the piano to your tuner unless you have it appraised by another "disinterested" piano technician.

But, before you advertise it for sale, Willa, have it tuned and have such repairs made as are necessary for each key to work properly (like, it's hard to get a good price for a dirty, misfiring automobile). If you're really honest, you'll show the tuner's inspection report to the prospective buyer and make some compromise in price to allow him to have it properly repaired.

Hopefully, the piano which you are finished with, will have lots of life and beauty left in it to make a good "starter" piano for some other eager family.

Doctor Piano

How Your Piano is Made...

Dear Doctor Piano,

I like the way you explain things about pianos. It helps me to understand them better. But, I was wondering: Who invented the piano?

Dot B.

Dear Dot,

I'm glad you like my letters. The piano is a wonderful musical instrument and there's a lot more to know about it.

In Italy, a man named Bartolomeo Cristofori invented the first piano in 1709. Its father was the clavichord and its grandfather, the harpsichord. The genius of the piano was that, unlike the harpsichord, it could be played soft and loud. Hence the name: Pianoforte which means soft/loud.

Gottfried Silberman in Germany made further improvements to the piano and, in 1747, Frederick the Great of Prussia commanded that the first performance on the new instrument be given by none other than Johann Sebastian Bach. Unfortunately, Bach was at an advanced age and died before much music could be composed especially for the pianoforte.

The early models all looked like grand pianos until, in 1801, John Hawkins, an American inventor, produced an instrument that saved space in the home by placing the strings vertically instead of horizontally. It was, of course, called the vertical or upright piano and our homes today are filled with cousins of this instrument.

Since its first appearance, the piano has grown larger and more sophisticated until today's instrument is a mechanical marvel. Its action contains about 4000 parts and the tension of its 230 odd strings totals nearly 20 tons.

If the violin is the Queen of instruments, the piano is King. Able to whisper like a flute and roar like an organ, the piano is an orchestra in itself. It even contains its own drums and chimes, harps and guitars. It is so simple that a child can finger a beautiful melody, yet so complicated that no pianist through the ages has ever exhausted its possibilities or fathomed its mysteries.

Long live the King!

Doctor Piano

Dear Doctor Piano,

I can't see inside our piano, but I am curious. What are pianos made of?

Shirley F.

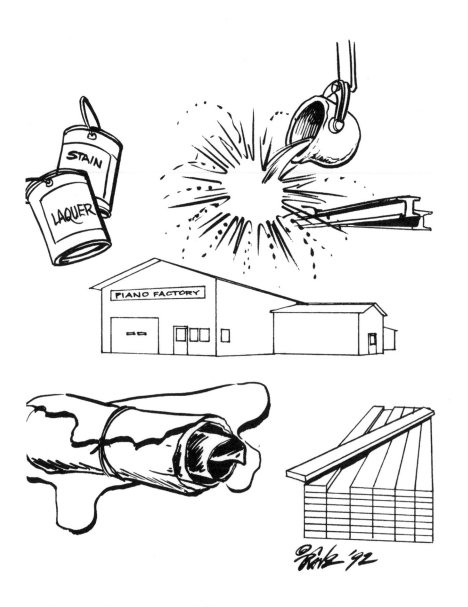

Dear Shirley,

I'm glad you're interested in your piano, inside and out. You've opened up an intriguing subject.

The parts you can see are made of some of the world's most beautiful woods: mahogany, walnut, oak and others. The keys are seldom made of ivory anymore since elephants are an endangered species. A plastic substitute works well.

Inside the piano, many more materials are to be found. Clear "hard rock" maple is used for the pin block which must hold the tuning pins tightly for many years. The wooden parts of the keys are made of a light material such as pine or bass wood. Many of the action parts are maple, a hard, compact wood. The most important wooden part of the piano is the soundboard which is constructed of slow grown spruce, a resonant material found in Alaska and other countries with cool climates.

For the tuning pins and strings, fine spring steel is used, often made in Germany. The backbone of the piano, the heavy metal plate, is poured from a special blend of cast iron. Bass strings are made by wrapping copper around a steel core to achieve weight and flexibility. In some pianos, aluminum rails are used to support the action, giving rigidity and freedom from warping. Even plastic appears in pianos—ABS plastic which resists weakening for many years and AS Resin which is almost indestructible. Rubber parts are seldom used because after a few years, they become brittle and must be replaced.

A great deal of felt is used in pianos: under the keys, between the strings and around the plate. The hammers are covered with very special compressed felt made from long fibre sheep wool.

The whole thing is held together by glue. Animal hide glue is still used to some extent but is giving way to modern glues which do not release their hold when attacked by moisture.

As you can see, Shirley, a fine piano is built from materials assembled from many parts of the world, machined and fitted together to produce the musical tones and resonance we enjoy so much.

A joy to own and a joy to play.

Doctor Piano

Dear Doctor Piano,

I suppose a piano is a stringed instrument like a guitar or a cello. But there are a lot of differences. Does a piano have resonance in the same way that a violin does?

Henry S.

Dear Henry,

Yes, in exactly the same way, though not many people realize it. And the resonance will grow with use as it does with other stringed instruments.

When a piano has a big loud sound, it's because it has lots of resonance. However, sometimes the big sound is raw and uncouth instead of being a cultured and controlled sound. So the quality of resonance also matters.

Resonance is partly due to the use of high quality wood but more important is the quality of the workmanship. However, even then, resonance can't be taken for granted.

Several years ago, I visited a violin maker. He told me that until a violin is totally completed, fitted with strings and played, he never knows if it'll be a good one. It might have a thin, shallow sound or it might have a rich resonant tone. And–the value depends on the resonance! The shallow one might go for $900, but the resonant one will bring $4000!

Pianos are much the same. With some manufacturers, two pianos off the same assembly line can be worlds apart in their sound. But, in contrast to the making of violins, the price of the two will be the same. With other manufacturers who build very fine pianos, there'll be much more uniformity of sound.

All of this has great significance for you if you're planning to purchase a new piano. There are beautiful, resonant instruments to be discovered and poor sounding ones to be avoided.

When you go shopping, take someone with you who really understands resonance and beauty of tone. And, when you've chosen a treasure, make a note of the serial number to be sure the same one is delivered to your home.

Doctor Piano

Dear Doctor Piano,

My friend and I tried to move my piano just a few feet but we could hardly budge it. It's not very big. Why is it so terribly heavy?

Muriel H.

Dear Muriel,

I know what you mean. When you try to move one, it seems like somebody nailed it to the floor.

The main reason behind all that weight is rigidity. The structure of the piano must be rigid and unmoving in order to stay in tune.

Look at it this way, Muriel. Each string in the piano is stretched at about 165 pounds. There are about 230 of them and that makes a total of 37,950 pounds of tension—nearly 19 tons! That's enough pull to lift your house right off its foundation!

This huge amount of stress on the piano's frame demands an extremely solid structure. The slightest warping or weakening will throw it wildly out of tune, rendering it useless as a musical instrument.

As a result, piano manufacturers install a thick cast iron plate to hold the strings and support it well with a heavy wooden frame often containing several sturdy hardwood posts.

You see then, Muriel, that it can't be helped. If you want a piano that'll sound beautiful and stay well in tune, you have to have one that takes four men to move it. There's no way around it.

Doctor Piano

Dear Doctor Piano,

Our piano needs to be moved down to our basement. Piano movers charge so much. Can't I just get some guys to help me and do it myself?

Doug T.

Dear Doug,

Yes Doug, you can – if you don't value your piano – or your stairs – or your walls – or your friends.

The trouble is: A piano is so awkward and so heavy that it almost always gets away on you, especially going through doorways.

Suddenly, while you're straining away, somebody says, "Uh, oh". You'd better close your eyes and reach for your wallet. Half the paint off the doorjamb is now on the front of your piano.

Then, you have two choices – live with a damaged piano or get it fixed. And if you think the movers charge a lot, just try hiring a refinisher!

By the way, Doug, d'you want to know why piano movers charge quite a bit? Because, even though they have good trucks and hoists and ramps and dollies (all expensive), a scratch can happen to them, too. Then you, the owner, say, "You broke it, you fix it." So the movers have to get the refinisher.

It's a risky business. But you're a lot further ahead to let someone else take the risks, even if it costs.

Doctor Piano

Dear Doctor Piano,

I know that a lot of dust collects inside our piano. I've seen it when the tuner was here. It bugs me just to think of it sitting in there. Could you show me how to open up my piano so that I can clean it inside?

Ruby L.

Dear Ruby,

I know it's in there but we have another problem: disturbing the inside of the piano.

I feel like saying what the doctors say when someone asks what they should use to scrape the wax out of their ears: "The only thing you should put in your ear is your elbow with a towel wrapped around it."

It's sort of the same with pianos. There are a lot of tiny, delicate parts inside your piano which have been carefully adjusted to work properly. They can be easily damaged or knocked out of adjustment by a vacuum cleaner nozzle or even a dust cloth.

I really try to discourage people from reaching inside their pianos. It's not because I want them to call me so that I can charge another fee for a house call; it's because of the damage that can be done so easily. Even retrieving a pencil or eraser that has fallen into the action can cause the hammer butt springs to be bent or pushed out of their grooves. Vacuuming or dusting the action would be even worse.

Just wait for your favorite tuner to make his regular visit. Bring out the vacuum and ask him to clean the piano. He won't mind, though he may charge extra for his time. And, if he knocks something out of adjustment, he knows how to put it back.

Doctor Piano

Dear Doctor Piano,

I know that pianos are very old, probably 300 years. With all the technology we have developed in the 1990's, what new developments are happening in the area of pianos?

Bruce F.

Dear Bruce,

A lot of very exciting things are happening.

Player pianos are being made again. Not the old kind with paper rolls where every note sounded the same, but new technologies using computers. They're so sophisticated that every note is reproduced with exactly the proper touch and volume. Not only that, but a pupil can play his recital piece on one of these pianos, touch a button, then sit back and listen as the piano replays exactly what he played, including every nuance of touch and timing. And all of this in an acoustic piano!

Electronic pianos aren't so new but are useful for a casual player. Their actions are becoming more like that of a "real" piano and less like an organ. The tones are much more realistic and, on some models, you can choose between the sound of a larger or smaller grand piano or even that of an older upright piano. The loudspeaker is still there, so the realism isn't perfect, but electronic pianos are quite worthwhile.

Acoustic pianos with "midi" capability are excitingly new. Now, all those interesting synthesizer sounds can be added to the tones of an upright or grand piano. Some companies are even manufacturing an "add-on" midi attachment. Installing it will permit your present piano to produce organ and synthesizer sounds.

Bruce, an exciting new change is the development of an improved upright piano action. After nearly 100 years without significant changes, some startling new modifications have been made. This new action largely achieves the superior responsiveness and control previously associated only with grand pianos. Before long, you should be able to purchase pianos equipped with this improved action. Efforts are also being made to see if it's possible to incorporate these modifications into your present piano action. At last, the misnomer "Upright Grand" will take on some meaning.

Yes, Bruce, the piano industry is coming up with lots of new developments to enhance the joy and beauty of piano music.

Doctor Piano

Dear Doctor Piano,

I have an old piano, maybe it's an antique. But, I don't know exactly how old it is. Can you help me find out my piano's age?

Frank M.

Dear Frank,

It's a bit of a problem. The date that you can see moulded into the iron plate inside your piano refers to the date of the patent, not the manufacture, and usually that's the only date to be seen.

Come to think of it, cars are the same. They don't mark them with the date they left the factory. If you don't have the original bill of sale or if you can't tell by the style, you must find the serial number and have the dealer look up the model year from that.

The solution is the same for cars and pianos: the serial number. To find the age of your piano, call your favorite tuner and tell him the make of your piano and the serial number (usually stamped on the gold colored plate inside.) He has an atlas which lists the serial numbers and the dates of manufacture and he'll be able to tell you the year when your piano was built.

Then, you can say, "Gee, I didn't know it was that old!" and you can appreciate it even more.

Doctor Piano

Dear Doctor Piano,

I guess I don't understand much about pianos. They seem very confusing to me. I heard you say that there are 230 strings in a piano and yet I know there are only 88 keys. How come?

Brenda J.

Dear Brenda,

Perhaps I can clear up some of the confusion for you. Harps or harpsichords have only one string for each note. This works for them because their bridges and soundboards are very light and easy to set in motion. But, as a result, you'll notice that the sound is small and delicate.

A piano, however, is a powerful instrument. The soundboard and bridges are fairly stiff and heavy. A single string for each note would not vibrate them sufficiently to produce the glorious tone we love to hear.

I'll show you what the builders have done. If you can, Brenda, peek inside your upright or grand piano. Look at the strings close to the lowest notes on the piano. See how thick and heavy they look with copper wire wound around them? They're heavy enough to vibrate the soundboard by themselves, so one per note is sufficient. Notice that each felt hammer strikes only one of them.

Moving a little toward the centre of the piano, you'll see some strings that are not as thick though still wound with copper. Each hammer strikes two of them. The piano builders have found that it takes two of these strings tuned in unison to provide enough vibration for the soundboard.

Now, if you look on toward the right side of the piano, you'll see that all the strings are arranged in groups of three, each group struck by one felt hammer. In this area of the piano, it takes three strings tuned to the same note to move the soundboard sufficiently to bring out the tone.

Each group of strings which makes one musical note, whether one, two or three, is called a "unison". So, because there are 88 keys and 88 notes in a piano, there are 88 unisons, but at the same time–about 230 strings. Make sense now, Brenda?

Doctor Piano

Dear Doctor Piano,

I've heard that some pianos today are being made with plywood or "multi-layer" soundboards. Is this a good idea?

Barb M.

Dear Barb,

In some ways, yes, and in other ways, no.

First, what is the soundboard in a piano? It's that sheet of wood with diagonal ribs glued to it, which you can see from the back of the piano. It's about 5/16 of an inch thick and the bridges and strings are fastened to it on the other side. It functions as a mechanical loudspeaker for the piano, amplifying the sounds of the strings as they're played.

A plywood soundboard is good because it will not crack in extremely dry conditions as single-layer soundboards sometimes do. It may also be true that it'll resist more of the soundboard's shifting, due to humidity changes, which puts pianos out of tune.

But a plywood soundboard is sometimes used as a low cost, second-best solution for pianos. The job of amplifying the sounds of the strings is a tremendous responsibility. Because of this, the wood must be as resonant and responsive as possible. All over the world, piano makers have traditionally used a single layer of close-grained spruce for the best performance. (The same wood is used in violins.)

However, Barb, the increasing scarcity of good spruce softwoods and the availability of better gluing techniques are making changes necessary and possible. High quality multi-layer soundboards have been developed which equal the traditional spruce board in tuning stability, sustain quality and power.

These new soundboards are actually more expensive than traditional ones but it's always that way, isn't it? Progress never comes cheap.

Doctor Piano

Dear Doctor Piano,

There are a lot of notes in my piano that don't stop ringing when I release the keys. Are they supposed to do that?

Lori B.

Dear Lori,

I think you mean the notes near the top or right hand of the piano. Yes, they're supposed to do that and for a very good reason.

All pianos have dampers which stop the sound when the keys are released. However, piano manufacturers never put any dampers on the top 20 or 25 notes. In a piano with a lot of resonance, those notes go on ringing loudly and you wonder if they shouldn't have dampers also.

The reason they don't is "sympathetic resonance". This high-falutin' term simply means that when you play a note on your piano, any strings that aren't dampened will resonate and echo the same sound.

Try it for yourself, Lori. Go to your piano and step on the damper or sustain pedal (the right one). Now strike a single note in the center of the piano and listen. You'll hear all the other strings pick up sounds from the note you struck and echo them. The combined sound is much louder than the note you played. Isn't that wild?

Piano makers do the same thing in the extreme treble. They try everything they can to boost the sound of those high notes because their strings are so short that they don't have much volume. (The shortest is about 2 inches.)

So if they leave the dampers off the top two octaves, those strings will echo the high notes and make them sound louder. They'll also echo the high frequencies of lower notes and give the piano more brilliance. And you know what? It works!

Those people really know what they're doing, don't they?

Doctor Piano

Dear Doctor Piano,

As I've been listening to some pianos lately, I've been surprised at the differences in sound. And not all the differences are good. Can you tell me why the new little pianos sound so tinny?

Brent M.

Dear Brent,

Not all of them do, but enough that it's a problem.

Tinny sounds are caused by four things: Poor materials used in construction, poor workmanship in the factory, use of piano strings that are too short and poor servicing after the piano is in use.

The first three can be avoided by buying the best quality, highest priced piano you can afford. That little 36-inch spinet may be a doll of a piano but—tinny. As with purchasing all musical instruments, attempts to save money usually bring regrets later on.

And, of course, hire the best piano technician you can find to service your piano. He can usually correct much of the tinny sound.

What happens is this: the felt hammers become too hard or go out of shape as a result of constantly hitting the strings. A good piano tuner knows how to re-shape the hammers and soften them so that the tone will be much sweeter and more mellow.

However, if too many corners were cut in the manufacturing of your piano, even the best piano technician will be unable to make it sound truly beautiful.

So, don't be too hard on the poor guy.

Doctor Piano

Dear Doctor Piano,

Some of our friends' pianos have three pedals and ours only has two. Could you explain what the pedals do? Aren't they the same on every piano?

Larry B.

Dear Larry,

No, they're not always the same. Two of them are standard on every piano but the third, the middle pedal, could be anything.

The right pedal is always the "sustaining" or "damper" pedal. It lifts the dampers from the strings so that any notes that are struck will continue to sound until the pedal is released again.

The left pedal is always the "soft" pedal. In upright pianos, it moves the hammers closer to the strings so they strike with less force. In grands, depressing the left pedal moves the action and keys slightly to the right so the hammers strike only two of the three strings for each note. They also strike the single bass strings off-centre so that the whole volume of the piano is reduced.

These two are the really essential pedals and some pianos, like yours, Larry, have only two. But I'll tell you a funny thing: On many makes of pianos, the third pedal (the middle one) is there only because so many people think a proper piano should have 3 pedals. It does no more than the left one or, sometimes, it repeats part of the work of the right one or left one.

In most grands and a few high quality uprights, the centre pedal is a "sostenuto". It sustains the notes which are being held down at the moment it is depressed but not those played after. It's tricky to use but it can produce some beautiful effects.

In many upright pianos, the centre pedal is a "muffler" or "practice" pedal. When it is pressed, it lowers a strip of felt between the hammers and strings of the piano. It's not for playing music because it doesn't let enough of the piano's beautiful sound come through.

It's for playing those scales, chords and arpeggios that are a part of every day's practice sessions. They need to be played at full volume to develop the pianist's hands – producing power, flexibility, accuracy and fluidity in piano playing.

But you realize, scales at full volume do not soothe the savage beast. Mom may have a headache, Dad is on edge about his job, brother is trying to watch TV in the next room, sister is on the phone and the baby is sleeping. If you have one, lock down the practice pedal and give your technique a real workout. Won't your teacher be happy?

Piano teachers will tell you: the "sustaining" pedal is used too much, the "soft" pedal is used too little and beginners shouldn't use the pedals at all.

I hope this clears up the matter for you, Larry. *Keep pedalling!*

Doctor Piano

Dear Doctor Piano,

I've noticed something about my piano and others that I've listened to. The lowest notes have a lot of volume, the centre ones are kind of average and the highest notes are very soft. Why is this? Do the highest notes need to have such a weak sound?

Crispina K.

Dear Crispina,

What an observant question! Yes, I know what you mean. In some pianos you can hardly hear those high notes. And, let me tell you, they're almost impossible to tune.

There are reasons why they sound so faint. Some are inevitable reasons and others are the result of poor workmanship.

If you look inside your piano, you'll see that the lowest strings are thick and long. Lots of volume there. But now, look at the highest strings. See how short they are? The speaking length of the shortest one is about two inches and that's the cause of all the trouble. Those strings are so short and so light that they can't vibrate the upper bridge and soundboard sufficiently to achieve full volume and tone.

But there's something else. For proper sound, a piano string must be struck by the felt hammer about 1/7 of its length from the end. When you've only got two inches to work with, it isn't easy to get it exactly right.

So you can expect that some makers of pianos will succeed better than others. The high notes in some pianos will sound clearer and more resonant than some others. As a matter of fact, some people play these notes as a test of the quality of the piano's construction. Actually, it's not such a bad idea.

Doctor Piano

Tuning the Piano...

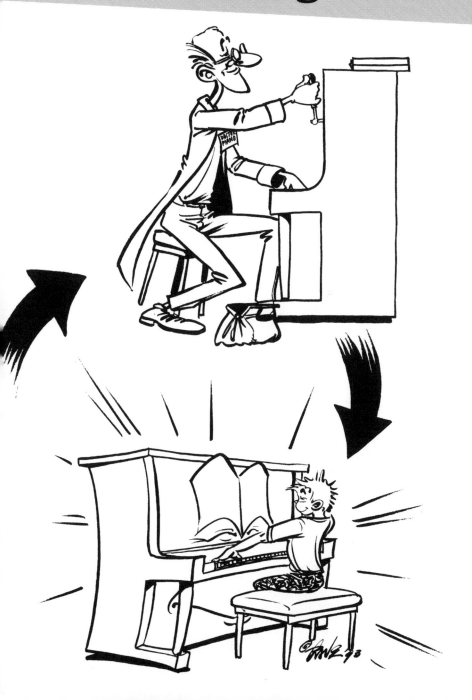

Dear Doctor Piano,

I always thought pianos stayed in tune for years. Now, I hear that they should be tuned every year or every six months or even sooner. I'm curious. How long will a piano stay in tune?

Grant J.

Dear Grant,

Are you ready for a shocker? Here it comes: Your piano will go slightly out of tune within 24 hours! You can't notice it nor can your piano teacher but a good piano tuner can.

Changes in the moisture content of the air in your home (the relative humidity) cause your piano to be shifting constantly in pitch and tuning.

But here's the good news: the changes are usually so slight that a good piano will keep sounding quite sweet and harmonious for a long time. Then, eventually the continual shifting and changing that's going on inside the piano will cause enough out-of-tuneness that you have to call your favorite tuner and have him sweeten it up again.

Some people don't mind the gradual deterioration of sound and will have the piano tuned each year (or—horrors!—even longer). Others like to have the piano sounding more perfect and have it tuned twice a year. And some others, who are really after pure sounds, set up an arrangement with their tuners to tune the piano three or four times a year—or even more.

That's the story, Grant. What's your choice?

Doctor Piano

Dear Doctor Piano,

Why do pianos go out of tune anyway? The thing sits there while the kids pound away on it and then somebody says, "It needs to be tuned." How come? It was all right yesterday.

David A.

Dear David,

The whole trouble is the soundboard – the large flat sheet of wood which you can see from the back of the piano. It's quite thin and flexible because, like a stereo loudspeaker, it has to vibrate and amplify the sound of the piano's strings. In good pianos, it's made of a single layer of close-grained spruce.

Because wood swells with extra moisture in the air and shrinks when the air gets drier, the soundboard is changing all the time. Unfortunately, the piano strings are hooked to it, so the tuning of the strings is also changing slightly all the time.

A rainy day will cause your piano to sound slightly off. So will: taking a shower, running the dishwasher or boiling the kettle. A cold snap in the winter makes a lot of difference. If the power humidifier on your furnace quits, your piano will start to scream. A flooded basement will make *you* scream for the piano tuner right away.

The two biggest changes during the year are: 1. When the furnace starts to dry out the air in the fall and 2. When the spring rains start. Lots of people have their pianos tuned right after these two variations in humidity.

Most of the changes in your piano are so subtle that you don't notice what's happening. But, gradually, it shifts out of tune until finally somebody says, "Hey, this piano sounds terrible!"

Time to call for your favorite piano tuner.

Doctor Piano

Dear Doctor Piano,

Pianos are really a mystery to me. I can't understand why they change so much. You'd think that when they are tuned, they'd stay that way. What makes them so unstable?

Alex G.

Dear Alex,

This is rather a technical subject, but a very important one, so I'll try to give you a clear understanding of it. If we can achieve stability in a piano, it'll stay in tune for a long time. If not, it'll go out quickly and always sound "sour".

When you consider that the heart of a piano is 230 steel strings stretched tightly over a thin, flexible wooden membrane (the soundboard), you begin to realize the difficulty of achieving stability.

Three factors affect the piano's stability or equilibrium:

1. Construction
2. Temperature and humidity changes
3. Tuning

Alex, to make this clearer, I want you to build a toy house in the bathtub (in actuality or in your imagination.) Take along a box of your child's wooden building blocks.

Fill the bathtub with about a foot of water and wait for it to become calm. The waves represent the changing temperature and humidity conditions surrounding your piano.

Start by laying a flat board (a foot square) on the water. This is your foundation. Now, use lots of blocks on top to make walls and partitions. Don't worry about a roof. You'll notice that every time you add another block, its weight makes the whole structure tip and sink. This is the effect of tuning on piano stability.

When you've finished building your "house upon the water", you may have placed more blocks near one edge and as a result, the whole thing is tipped and threatening to collapse. This, of course, represents poor construction and shows the instability caused by it.

Now, Alex, let's deal with each of the three factors. To make sure you have a piano constructed for good tuning stability, purchase the highest quality piano you can afford – the one with the best reputation as a great piano.

Second, see to it that the temperature and humidity conditions in your home are as constant as possible. Don't fiddle with the thermostat. Have a good quality furnace humidifier installed by your plumber. Or, he may recommend a de-humidifier. This will keep the "waves" from upsetting your piano's sound.

Third, have the piano tuned frequently – at least once a year. Tuning a piano always destabilizes it. Adding a large block makes the toy house tip a lot but adding a very small block hardly moves it at all. That's like the effect of tuning the piano. If it's very much out of tune, the tuner has to make large changes which destabilize the piano a lot. The whole structure of the piano has to readjust to the new tensions and find its equilibrium again (going out of tune in the process). But if the piano is only slightly out of tune, the changes made by the tuner are very tiny and the resulting instability is negligible.

This is the most important secret of having a stable piano that always sounds beautiful: Have it tuned regularly – BEFORE IT GOES SERIOUSLY OUT OF TUNE! Stability achieved.

Doctor Piano

Dear Doctor Piano,

I'm really a careful person when looking after equipment but sometimes I let things slide. What happens if I neglect to service my piano?

Jim F.

Dear Jim,

Watch it! I may report you to *The Society For Prevention Of Cruelty To Pianos And Their Families!*

Actually, it's a bit like neglecting to service your car. You don't notice much difference at first, but eventually that dirty oil takes its toll. Engine parts begin to wear much quicker than normal. Before long, you have a car that's old before its time.

Something the same happens with pianos. The first thing is that the piano will go out of tune and sound "ringy" or "weird". This means that the string tension is dropping. Now, other instruments will not harmonize with it. After some years, the piano may be a quarter or a half-tone flat. Raising it back up is not hard for the tuner, but it is hard on the piano. Strings may break or cracks appear in the bridges.

Jim, if the piano is neglected for more years, changes will occur in the action. The keys will feel loose, the hammers will not strike properly and the tone will become weak and shrill.

Some pianos can handle neglect better than others. *But why take the chance?* Call your favorite tuner and have him come on a regular basis.

"A well-tuned piano is a thing of beauty."

Doctor Piano

Dear Doctor Piano,

What's the matter with my piano? It still sounds like a piano but the beauty has gone out of it.

Robert Pounder

Dear Robert,

What a perceptive question! You must be a very sensitive person to realize that a piano can have beauty separate from just "sounding like a piano". It's like someone playing a cheap violin: you hear the notes, you know it's a violin, but there's no beauty there.

Let me place another question alongside yours:

"How can a child learn to play beautiful music on a piano that is incapable of producing beauty?"

Beauty in a piano refers to resonant tone–a mellow but rich quality of sound that's full of overtones but free from harshness.

Several things cause lack of beauty in a piano:

CHEAP CONSTRUCTION. There never was any beauty in it in the first place.

POOR ACTION REGULATION. An action which is out of adjustment cannot bring beauty of tone from even a good quality piano.

NEGLECTED TUNING. The most common cause and the easiest one to remedy.

OLD AGE. When the hammers are hardened, the strings are crystallized and the soundboard is flat, beauty has fled.

Robert, some of these things can be repaired. But for others, it's not possible or feasible because of excessive cost. Call your favorite piano tuner. He can tell you how the beauty can be restored to your piano, or failing that, how to find one with beauty in it.

Doctor Piano

Dear Doctor Piano,

We have a beautiful piano with a gorgeous tone and we're trying to take care of it properly. How often should we have it tuned?

Marcelle G.

Dear Marcelle,

The quick answer is, "It depends how fussy you are." It's like having your hair permed (how perfect do you want your hair to look?) or like having your car serviced (how perfectly smooth do you want the motor to run?)

The same with your piano: How perfectly smooth and clear and harmonious do you want your piano to sound?

But, there's a catch. You may have been brought up in a home where the piano was seldom tuned and it's difficult for you to tell when the clarity and purity slips out of your piano.

Here's a quick test: Go to the piano and strike a single note or an octave. Listen hard. If you hear the sound moving or turning or changing in volume (a slow *wah, wah, wah*), the note or octave is out of tune and so, probably, is the whole piano. An in-tune note or octave sounds straight and still, no moving or fluctuating at all.

Warning: Don't try this test with other combinations of notes because they're supposed to have moving sounds when they're in tune. When testing chords, listen for sweetness or sourness to determine the condition of the tuning.

Rule of thumb: Your piano should be tuned every year in order to keep it sounding pleasant. If you want it to sound more perfect, ask your favorite tuner to do it twice a year, April and October or more often than that.(Actually, it's a good plan to have the piano tuned most often during the portion of the year when you use it the most.)

By keeping your piano well tuned, you're helping your children to learn to recognize and to produce beauty in musical sounds.

I hope this answers your question, Marcelle.

Doctor Piano

Dear Doctor Piano,

I don't know much about music, so I depend on my nine-year-old daughter to tell me when the piano needs tuning. About this "regulation" you talk about which will make the piano "feel" better: Will my child notice the difference?

Jeri M.

Dear Jeri,

The other day, I heard that question somewhere else and, to tell you the truth–I didn't like it very much.

The scene was this: I was in a home, tuning the piano. I noticed that some parts of the action were out of adjustment. The keys still played and a beginner might not notice that anything was wrong. But I knew that the keys and action parts weren't moving correctly and that two unfortunate results would occur:

1. Some of the fine points of piano technique could never be practised on this piano because the action couldn't perform them.

2. No young pianist practicing on this piano could ever develop a feel for correct piano touch.

Knowing these things, I mentioned the need for action adjustments to the lady of the house. That's when she said it: "*Will my child notice the difference?*"

My first reaction was, "What does that have to do with the price of tea in China?" (But I didn't say it out loud!) I have to admit I was a bit "ticked off". I was thinking things like: "Is this child an authority on correct piano action and tuning?" "Why should an experienced piano technician's word be challenged and a beginning piano pupil's word be accepted?" I was probably over-reacting.

After a moment, I tried to make clear to the lady that a standard is a standard. Either the piano performs correctly or it doesn't–regardless of who notices the difference.

Jeri, when you drive up to the service station and ask the attendant to check the air pressure in the tires, you don't say, "Will I notice the difference?" There's a correct tire pressure for your car and there's a correct standard of action regulation for your piano.

As a matter of fact, people notice lots of wrong things and call them right. I had a customer once who was disappointed in my tuning because I had taken the "nice ringy sound" out of the piano. She didn't realize that the "ringy" sound was the sign of out-of-tuneness. She'd become so accustomed to the sound of her piano when it was out of tune that when it was put in tune–she thought it was wrong.

I guess what it comes down to is this: When you have a qualified, conscientious piano technician, you need to trust his judgment. If you let him, he'll bring your piano to the highest standard of touch and tone which it's capable of producing. It may cost you some money but you'll have an instrument by which your child can judge all others.

Doctor Piano

Dear Doctor Piano,

I don't have a very good ear for music and the piano always seems to sound pretty much the same to me from one year to the next. Is there some way that I can tell if my piano needs tuning?

Emily M.

Dear Emily,

I appreciate your desire to become more sensitive to the sounds of your piano. Some parents just wait for their children to complain before deciding that tuning is needed. Others do not realize their piano is out of tune until a piano teacher or other musician tells them.

Well, let me be the first to tell you–you can discover for yourself if your piano needs tuning. Simply answer these 2 easy questions:

1. *Does it sound bad?* To discover this, go to the piano and play an octave–middle C with the C below. Strike the two notes at the same time, hold them down and listen. If the musical sound seems sour to you or if the sound seems to be "moving", "turning" or "vibrating", the octave is out of tune and so, probably, is the rest of the piano.

2. *Has it been a year since it was tuned?* Seasonal humidity changes are the cause of out-of-tuneness in a piano. By the time a year goes by–fall, winter, spring and summer–your piano will be out of tune.

Wasn't that easy, Emily? If the answer to either of these questions is *Yes,* it's time to call your favorite tuner.

When he comes, ask him to demonstrate the sounds of out-of-tune notes for you. Then, you'll be able to hear them more easily next time.

Doctor Piano

Dear Doctor Piano,

My tuner always uses the term "A440". I know that it has something to do with the pitch of the piano, but that's all. Could you explain it to me?"

B.J.H.

Dear B.J.

Certainly. 440 is the number of vibrations per second of the A above Middle C. It's significant because the frequency of this note has been made the international standard for all instruments.

After centuries of individual and haphazard choices of pitch references, 440 Hertz (vibrations per second) was adopted as the standard for A above Middle C. This means that all pianos, organs, accordions, brass instruments, woodwinds and string instruments are built to A440. Because of this, all these instruments can be played together harmoniously.

There are a few rebels. Some orchestras feel that a higher pitch will give a more brilliant sound to the string section and they move up to A442 or even A444.

If your piano is tuned to A440, it'll match any other instruments brought into your home and will be a beautiful assistance in group playing.

However, if it's been too long since your piano was tuned, the pitch may have fallen to A435 or A425 (1/4 tone flat) or even A410 (1/2 tone flat.) This happens because seasonal fluctuations in humidity always push the pitch of the piano down.

When it's like this, instead of sweet harmony with other instruments, you'll hear only sour discords.

Your favorite tuner knows how to bring the pitch of the piano back up to the standard of A440. And, if you arrange with him to tune your piano on a regular basis, he'll keep it there.

Here's to harmony. A440 forever!

Doctor Piano

Dear Doctor Piano,

I have to admit that it's been quite a while since our piano was tuned and I knew it was sounding pretty bad. But why did my tuner tell me he has to raise the pitch of my piano?

Helen P.

Dear Helen,

I'm sorry to have to say it, but if he tells you this, it's probably your fault.

Pianos usually creep downwards in pitch. This is caused by stretching of the strings, flattening of the soundboard and minute compression of the general structure.

Almost every time your piano is tuned, the tuner has to bring up the pitch slightly– anywhere from 2% to 12% of a half tone. He makes this a part of his tuning procedure and doesn't charge you extra for it.

However, if the piano's been moved from a damp climate to a dry one or if it's been neglected, that is, allowed to go 2 years or more without tuning (1 year for a new piano), the pitch will have dropped so much that extra pitch-raising work has to be done. It may be 15% to 50% low or more.

If the tuner tries to raise the pitch and fine-tune the piano in one operation, the piano will shift out of tune immediately. He first has to go over the entire piano, tightening all the strings to bring them up to standard pitch and he may charge $15 to $30 for this operation. Only then can he bring the piano to reasonable in-tuneness and he'll add the usual tuning fee to the previous amount.(Because of the instability caused by raising the pitch, a concert level of tuning is impossible until later.)

Another thing: It's possible that a string may break during this tightening process. Your tuner can repair it easily but it adds to the expense. There's also a very remote possibility that the plate may crack as a result of the restored tensions–another hazard of the process.(See page 146 for further explanation)

But, Helen, we're not finished yet! The added pressures of the restored tightness may be as high as 2000 or 3000 pounds and the structure of the piano must shift and adjust to this change in stress. The process takes a few weeks before the piano stabilizes again. During this time the piano will shift somewhat out of tune.

Discouraging, isn't it? Here, you paid the man $80 or $100 and two weeks later the piano sounds raunchy again. As I told you, it's not his fault, it's the piano's–or yours. He'll tell you it needs to be tuned again in six weeks and he's right. Make an appointment, have it tuned and pay him again.

Agonizing and expensive. So, don't let it happen. Keep the piano in good shape. Have it tuned regularly. OK?

Doctor Piano

Dear Doctor Piano,

When we had our piano serviced a while back, the tuner told us, "A piano has to be in tune before it can be tuned." That seemed like a strange thing to say. What did he mean?

Lorraine T.

Dear Lorraine,

It's a peculiar expression, alright, but there's a real meaning behind it.

The reality is that a piano is a set of tightly stretched steel strings which rest on a thin wooden membrane called the soundboard. It's a delicate balance of tension and flexibility. A slight increase in the tension of one string will reduce the tightness of neighboring strings.

Since you live on a farm, Lorraine, you may have experienced a similar situation in installing barbed wire fences: tightening one strand causes the others to suddenly go loose.

Realizing this helps you to appreciate why pianos go out of tune so easily. The soundboard is affected by humidity changes, the strings are affected by temperature changes and each one affects the others.

So, when a piano tuner comes to your home and finds your piano quite a bit out of tune, he has a special problem. If he starts right in to tune the piano, every time he tightens a string, the large increase in tension will cause the one just tuned to go out of tune again. If he tunes the whole piano in this way, it'll be distinctly out of tune when he's finished. What a bummer! If you notice it, you may ask him never to come back again.

The correct procedure is to carry out a pitch balancing operation first. It doesn't take long, but it's hard work and he needs to charge extra for doing it.

When this operation is finished, the piano will be at the correct overall string tension – almost in tune. *Now it can be tuned.* As each string is brought to its perfect position, the changes are so slight that other strings are little affected and the piano will be properly in tune when he's finished.

Now it makes sense, doesn't it, Lorraine?

Doctor Piano

Dear Doctor Piano,

We recently had our piano delivered to our house. I called the tuner and made an appointment. But, I've never done this before and I don't know what to expect. How long will it take him to tune our piano?

Gary K.

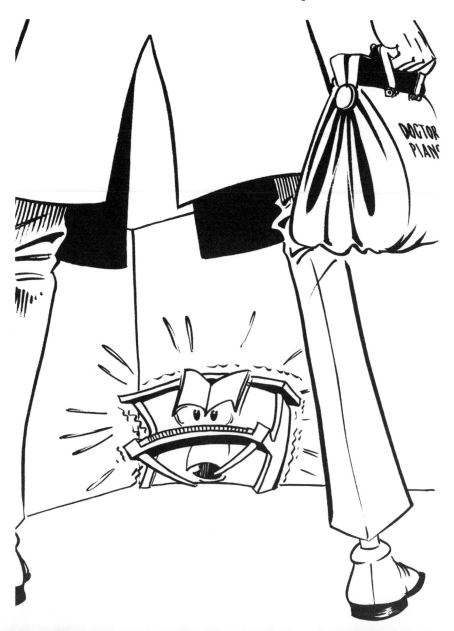

Dear Gary,

Many people are shocked to learn that it usually takes an hour and a half or two hours to service their piano. At least, it takes me that long. Maybe I'm too fussy, but I haven't been able to speed up very much even after years of experience.

It depends on how regularly a piano is tuned. If it's been six months or a year, each tuning pin needs to be turned only a tiny amount, which takes less time. If it's been longer since the last tuning, it's more difficult to set the pins. On top of that, the larger changes render the piano somewhat unstable. Strings tend to shift out of tune even while the tuner's working and have to be retuned. Time consuming.

It also depends on the tuner. With much experience, he learns to hear quickly and to set the tuning pins without any wasted motions. This makes the process quicker—perhaps an hour or a bit less. But let me warn you, Gary, if a tuner comes along who says he's finished in half an hour, better get a second opinion. It's possible, but such tuners are few and far between.

Tuning time also depends a lot on the piano. Some have strings that fall into place quickly and easily. Others are touchy and hard to tune; they almost seem to fight the tuning process. I find I have to be patient. If it fights me, I just have to struggle with it and coax it into place.

The important thing is—the job has to be done right, no matter how long it takes.

Doctor Piano

Dear Doctor Piano,

I dread it when the tuner comes to work on the piano. The sounds of tuning drive me up the wall. "Ping, ping, ping" for hours. What should I do while this is going on?

Rossana A.

Dear Rossana,

I have to admit it: it's a painful sound, all right.

I've had people do lots of different things: escape to the basement, vacuum in another part of the house, go to visit the neighbors, etc. I had one man sit on the sofa only 10 feet from the piano—and go to sleep! I don't know how he did it.

But, Rossana, what you should do if you want to understand your piano better, is—sit down and listen. Ask the tuner to explain what he's doing and listen to it. You won't be able to hear everything but you'll learn a lot.

Especially listen to the "beats" ("waves", "vibrations") disappearing. What you want to be able to hear is the difference between the "uneven", "wavy", "vibrating", "moving" sounds of out-of-tune notes as compared to the "smooth", "straight", "still" sounds of in-tune notes. Listen as the tuner makes a note all "wavy" then smooths it out to perfect tuning. See if you can hear them as he does this in every area of the piano: low, medium and high.

Right now, Rossana, you may say you can't tell if the piano is in tune or out of tune, but listening will change that. The more you listen, the more you'll come to recognize that beautiful, round, pure tone which a piano can produce when it's properly cared for.

And, if that happens, you'll have received a valuable bonus from the pain of listening to your piano tuner—and you didn't even have to pay for it!

Doctor Piano

Caring For Your Piano...

Dear Doctor Piano,

The piano man was here the other day. He was so friendly and helpful and he seemed to do a good job on the piano. It sounds beautiful to me. But one thing puzzled me. Why did he ask what level of music is being played on our piano?

Wendy P.

Dear Wendy,

He wants to make sure that your piano is ready to meet the demands you're going to place on it.

It's like your car. If you're driving three miles to and from work each day, that's one thing. But if you're planning a trip to Halifax, a tune-up probably isn't enough to get it ready. You may have to get it completely overhauled or even trade it in for a new one.

If you have a family member who plans to play Grade 6, 8 or 10 music on your piano, more than tuning may be required to prepare it. A high level of music requires a piano with an extremely responsive action and refined sense of touch.

Your piano may need the same treatment as your car: an overhaul—some adjustments and refinements to the action to make it respond more efficiently. Or some work may be required on the sound quality, to bring its tone up to the resonance and beauty needed for advanced music.

Much of this work is time-consuming and costly. Your favorite tuner may even recommend that you move up to a higher quality piano. Ouch! That hits the pocket book even harder.

But on the day when your child mounts the stage at the recital hall, sits down to the grand piano and pours out beautiful, heavenly music—it'll be worth it all. Right?

Doctor Piano

Dear Doctor Piano,

Just recently, my piano tuner told me that my piano needs "regulation" and that it will cost $200 to $400 or even more. Why did he do that? Is he just trying to make money?

Judy O.

Dear Judy,

Not necessarily. If he's conscientious, he's trying to alert you to the fact that some of the critical adjustments of your piano's action have shifted due to wear or changes in climatic conditions. It still plays, but looseness and inefficiency now characterize the action of your piano.

The touch has become sloppy and wasteful. The tone has become weak and thin. Some keys may not produce a sound at all, others may fail when played very softly or with quick repetition and still others may stick down when played.

Some hopeful little pupils are trying to learn their little pieces on this piano the way the teacher taught them but the piano won't let them. All of its faults frustrate their musical desires until the desires give in.

The action of a piano functions efficiently only when its parts are adjusted carefully to an accuracy sometimes measured in thousandths of an inch. Time-consuming work but necessary to achieving proper touch and tone in your piano.

Judy, your favorite tuner knows how to create this efficiency in your piano. He's not trying to take advantage of you. Let him go ahead and do it.

Doctor Piano

Dear Doctor Piano,

When my son played in the music festival recently, he said the piano felt different and it threw him off. What happened?

Barb C.

Dear Barb,

In all likelihood, the piano at the festival was maintained in good standard condition. Please forgive me if I get technical for a minute or two:

The keys moved down 3/8", the hammers travelled 3/4" toward the strings, lifted the dampers, then travelled another 3/4", released from the keys 1/8" from the strings, struck them and bounced back 5/8".

These dimensions are standard for almost all pianos, giving them a *touch* or *feel* which pianists get used to.

But perhaps, Barb, your piano hasn't been regulated for many years and the adjustments have shifted: The keys depress only 5/16", the hammers have to travel 1 1/4" before contacting the dampers, then they release from the keys 5/8" from the strings and bounce back 1 1/4". Your piano's hammers may also be too hard, producing too much sound with too little effort.

If this is the case, the piano will feel funny. But to a little boy who gets used to it this way, it will be the festival piano that feels funny and he won't be able to play his best.

Call your favorite piano tuner and ask him to make sure your piano is adjusted to standard dimensions.

One thing more. If your piano is a small, apartment-size upright and the festival piano is a grand, there are bound to be considerable differences in touch and sound in spite of careful regulation. Ask your piano teacher to make sure that your son has a chance to practice his piece on a larger piano before his festival performance.

I hope he has better success next time.

Doctor Piano

Dear Doctor Piano,

The piano teacher comes to our home and gives lessons to our seven-year-old. Lately, she's been telling me that the piano will not play properly at low volume. What causes the difficulty in making the notes sound in pianissimo playing? Can it be repaired?

Lyle B.

Dear Lyle,

This is one of the most common problems in pianos built in the last 35 years. And if an adult complains about it, think of the difficulty it creates for a child whose fingers are light and weak.

What happens is this: The piano teacher says, "Play these measures very softly." But as soon as the pupil tries, some of the notes fail to play. What frustration! After two or three misses that pupil won't even *try* to play softly.

Or it may be that the notes will sound on the teacher's piano but not on the one at home. More frustration! To avoid the embarrassment of notes failing to sound, the pupil will simply play loudly all the time. And the teacher's attempts to teach the technique of pianissimo playing go right out the window!

Yes, Lyle, this problem can be repaired but you need to bring it to the attention of your favorite piano tuner. When he makes his regular visits, he may be concentrating so much on the tuning that he fails to thoroughly check the regulation of the piano's action or the voicing of the hammers. Or he may hesitate to mention the problem because of the extra expense involved.

But if you mention the difficulty you're having with the keys, he'll give you an estimate of the work and cost required to properly "regulate the action". Then, when your child tries to play pianissimo – the piano will do it.

Doctor Piano

Dear Doctor Piano,

We are starting our children in piano lessons and we want to make sure everything is as ideal as possible for them. We have a good teacher but now I'm concerned. Is our piano good enough for what the teacher wants to teach our children?

Henry C.

Dear Henry,

I'm glad you're asking that question. In a lot of homes the answer is "No" and nobody realizes it.

Actually, I can only give part of the answer. I can tell the degree of musicianship which the piano can support, but I don't know the level of technique which the teacher desires.

Here's how you can get the complete answer to your question. (Some teachers may not like me for this, but if they're concerned about the musical growth of their pupils, they'll agree.)

Invite your piano teacher to your home for tea. While she's there, ask her to play your piano and pose the question you asked me. She may say, "This piano is very responsive and is fine for everything I want to teach."

Or she may say, "I cannot make this piano respond to the technique I am trying to teach your children. They cannot learn properly on this piano as it is now."

You may have a piano teacher who comes to your home and teaches on your piano, but don't take silence as approval. She may be thinking some things that she's afraid to say because needed improvements will cost you money. Ask her the question point blank so that you get her true opinion.

If you get negative answers about your piano or even doubtful answers, don't take any chances. Call your favorite piano tuner and ask him if he can improve the piano to meet the standards set by your piano teacher.

You may get a pleasant surprise. He may be able to restore the needed responsiveness at a very reasonable cost. Or, regretfully, he may inform you that you'll never have a suitable instrument unless you trade it in for a better one. Not very nice news but you can't correct a problem unless you know the truth.

I hope this helps, Henry.

Doctor Piano

Dear Doctor Piano,

A while ago, a tuner told me that my piano was a piece of junk. That really bothered me. How should I react?

Keith S.

Dear Keith,

I hope he wasn't referring to a cherished heirloom passed on to you by your grandmother.

It surprises me how many times I hear this complaint. It surprises me even more that any piano tuner would say such a thing. Great bedside manner, eh?

Have you ever had a mechanic say that about your car when you went in for servicing? Of course not. If he had, he'd lose a customer (more than that if his boss found out).

Probably that uncouth tuner was trying to get the point across that if we hope to have our children learn to hear and to love and to produce beauty in piano music, we parents must provide instruments that are capable of beauty.

But even if the piano is rather worthless, there's a better way to say it. He should have said, "Mrs. Jones, when your children start to show real interest in music, you probably should think of trading this piano for a better one." (Actually, it's already a discouragement to the kids, but maybe she'll take the hint.)

When I think about it, Keith, I haven't been saying this to people often enough. Too many prospective musicians have to struggle through lessons, practicing on a piano that sounds as sour as a pickle and plays like a worn out eggbeater.

How should you react when some unfeeling tuner comes out with such discourteous criticism? Try not to get angry. Try to ignore his rudeness because he may be telling you the truth. Thank him. Then call another tuner and get a second opinion.

Doctor Piano

Dear Doctor Piano,

The best piano I have been able to afford is an older one. It has a beautiful tone but it's had a lot of use. The keys seem kind of loose and hard to control. Can the keys on my piano be made heavier to press?

Hannah E.

Dear Hannah,

That seems like a strange question, but I know why you're asking it. You're an advanced piano student and you want your piano to provide the kind of resistance which will make your fingers strong. A lot of older pianos have become so loose and easy to play that they don't provide the needed exercise.

Actually, Hannah, it's difficult to alter the touch of a piano to any great extent, but some changes can be made. I know a mother who placed some home-made weights inside the piano for her daughter's benefit. It ruined the responsiveness of the piano but it certainly provided resistance.

Changes can be made in three ways: adjusting or rebuilding the action, softening the tone of the hammers and weighting the keys. Probably one or more of these approaches will accomplish what you need. The important thing is to make changes cautiously, allowing time in between for the pianist to sense the differences in touch. It's important, too, to be sure that each change can be reversed if it proves unsatisfactory later on.

Your favorite tuner has sensitivity to piano touch and tone and the experience in action regulating which will help to arrive at the weight and feel which will suit your requirements.

Doctor Piano

Dear Doctor Piano,

When I press the keys on my piano, they feel as though they move a ways before anything happens. What's wrong?

John M.

Dear John,

Good for you! You've correctly analyzed the problem. We call it "Lost Motion". What you've said is exactly what happens. A gap exists in the train of parts which connects the piano keys and the felt hammers which strike the strings. So when you slowly press a key, it moves with little resistance across the gap. Then you can feel the added weight as it touches and begins to move the hammer mechanism.

If the funny feel of the key was the only result of Lost Motion, we wouldn't worry much about it. But there's more. The presence of the gap means that the hammer mechanism is not being moved far enough (the reason for the name).

Several results occur which are too technical to try to describe here. But the end result is a loss of power in the piano and precision in the touch, making the piano feel and sound lousy.

A couple of things cause Lost Motion. Dryness in the house can shrink the wooden parts and cause the gap to appear. But the most serious cause is the years of playing the piano. The felt and leather parts become worn and packed down and the gap occurs. So you can see, John, the presence of Lost Motion may mean that these parts have outlived their usefulness.

Call your favorite tuner. This is a common problem in pianos and he knows what to do about it. Each key contains a screw which he'll adjust to remove the Lost Motion and he'll charge you $15 to $30. But before he does it, ask him if he feels that the parts need to be renewed.

When he's finished, John, you'll be amazed at how much better your piano will feel and sound.

Doctor Piano

Dear Doctor Piano,

I hate it when people talk in technical terms and don't explain what they mean. When the tuner was here, I didn't understand a thing he was talking about. He said the "let-off" adjustment in my piano is wrong. What does he mean?

Olga M.

Dear Olga,

He's talking about an adjustment in your piano's action which is critical in making the piano play easily and responsively. I'll try to explain it in everyday terms.

When you press a key on your piano, a felt hammer flies up and strikes the strings. The key and the hammer are connected by a little piece of wood or plastic called a "jack". The jack is designed so that just before the hammer contacts the strings, the connection is broken. This "let-off" is necessary so that the hammer is free to rebound, allowing the strings to sound.

But, if "let-off" occurs too early, the power and control of the pianist's fingers is disconnected from the hammers too soon. As a result, the piano can't be played as loudly or as softly as desired. In fact, when trying to play very softly, some hammers may completely fail to touch the strings—a most frustrating effect for the pianist.

To restore the lost efficiency of your piano's action, a corrective adjustment must be made to each of the 88 keys on the piano. It'll take your favorite tuner extra time to make this correction and it'll cost $25 to $50, but it's worth it. Your piano will feel and sound much like it did when it was brand new.

Doctor Piano

Dear Doctor Piano,

I think the most frustrating thing about a piano is when you press a key and nothing happens. It drives our children nearly crazy. What causes some of the keys on our piano to stick.?

Jerry F.

Dear Jerry,

This is a very common complaint. Dozens of things can cause sticking keys, all the way from a tight key bushing to a weak jack spring.

Other causes? Key slip too close, jack flange unglued, garbage in the action, worn wippen felt, improper key balance, hammer butt pins too tight, worn key buttons, broken key, rainy weather, etc, etc. See what I mean?

The trouble is, you can't fix most of these problems yourself. Look and see if a nickel or a piece of dirt is wedged between the sticking keys. If not, you're beat. Call your favorite tuner and hope the bill isn't too high.

And, Jerry, don't blame the poor guy if he charges you quite a bit. It may only take him 10 minutes to fix the piano but it may have taken him an hour to drive to your house and back. In that time he could've nearly tuned another piano for $75.00. He'll try to be fair with you but he has to make a living, too.

Of course, if you ask him to tune the piano at the same time, he probably won't even charge you for a simple repair.

Tell you what—bring out a hot cup of coffee and a big piece of chocolate cake. It never hurts to put him in a good mood.

Doctor Piano

Dear Doctor Piano,

A long time ago, a piano salesman cautioned us strongly to avoid placing drinking glasses or potted plants on the piano. He made it sound like a huge problem. Is it really that serious?

Donna S.

Dear Donna,

They always leak. Drinking glasses are always wet on the bottom and often they get knocked over. Plants always overflow when you water them.

The point is, liquid does huge damage to pianos. Rings and stains on the finish are hard to repair. But that's only the beginning. If the liquid gets inside, it does even more horrendous things.

Don't let it happen! It'll give lots of work to your piano tuner and make you a lot poorer, but worst of all, your piano may never be the same again.

The tuner looks inside and says, "Uh, oh!" The strings are rusted, some are broken. Hammers and dampers have hardened. Glue joints have come apart. Moving parts are sluggish and some are seized up. The bass strings, splashed with a sweet drink, have suffered an instant, irreversible loss of tone.

Yup! Lots of work for the tuner, poverty for you and permanent loss to the piano.

Doctor Piano

Dear Doctor Piano,

I notice that a lot of dust and dirt settles inside our piano. That surely doesn't do it any good. When the tuner comes and opens up my piano, should I get out the vacuum?

Velma M.

Dear Velma,

You've hit on a question that I'm asked almost every day.

The scenario is this: I've been invited into a home to tune the piano. When I take off the front board, the lady of the house suddenly sees the inevitable coating of dust inside the piano. Shocked and embarrassed, she quickly suggests getting out the vacuum cleaner.

I usually oblige and soon the offensive dust is safely inside the noisy machine. Maybe you've noticed: nothing thrills a housewife more than the sight of ugly dirt being eradicated.

Actually, though, very little good is accomplished by this vacuuming. A piano is so full of little bits and pieces that hardly any of the dust can be removed in this way. It just sits there and collects more as time goes by. Fortunately, the dust doesn't seem to harm the piano's action and it continues to perform efficiently for many years.

The only way to get rid of the dirt hiding in the many crevasses is to use compressed air to blow it out—hardly a desirable operation for a fastidious lady's home. Eventually though, the piano will be taken to a shop for rebuilding, an excellent time for a thorough cleaning.

In the meantime, Velma, don't worry about the cleanliness of your piano's interior. It's not going to make any difference and there's not much you can do about it anyway.

Doctor Piano

Dear Doctor Piano,

Our piano tuner is always doing something that I don't understand and I hate to stand there and ask him questions. The other day, he was replacing a broken string. When he put in the new string, he added a piece of felt so that it couldn't make any sound. Why?

Val W.

Dear Val,

I guess we tuners are mysterious creatures. I'm sorry.

But let me ask you a question: What happens when you put a new string on your guitar?

That's right, Val, it stretches and goes flat. It's a pain because, for several weeks, it seems like it's always out of tune and you have to keep cranking it up.

Exactly the same thing happens when a new string is installed in your piano. It stretches and goes out of tune. If you could afford it, you should have the tuner pull it up the very next day. But it would be flat again the day after that.

Your favorite tuner knows what a painful discord an out-of-tune string creates in a well-tuned piano, so he wedges a little piece of felt between the new one and its neighbor so that the offender can't be heard. Since a piano usually has more than one string per note, playing the key will still cause a string to sound, one that stays in tune. In this way the discords can be avoided.

The new string will keep on stretching and going out of tune for weeks, perhaps as long as a year. Then, when he returns again to tune the piano in six months or a year, the tuner will remove the felt, allowing the new string to sound again. By this time, the newcomer should have stretched enough so that it can take its place among the stable strings of a piano that stays beautifully in tune.

Doctor Piano

Dear Doctor Piano,

I know that guitar strings have to be replaced rather frequently because the tone goes out of them. Do piano strings ever have to be replaced?

Pam G.

Dear Pam,

Yes, that's one of the things that deteriorate as the piano grows older. Gradually, the steel of the strings hardens and they begin to lose their elasticity and tone. The sound becomes weak and thin.

Putting in a new set of strings will restore much of the volume and warmth of sound to the piano. But it's a big job; so big that, though it's a common operation for grands, it's seldom undertaken in uprights. This may change, though. New upright pianos have become so expensive that it's becoming practical to spend a thousand or two to rebuild a good old one.

The bass strings usually lose their beauty of tone first. But they're the easiest to replace, especially in a grand, so the cost isn't so high, about $300 - $500.(More for a larger grand)

The treble strings are another story. Because it's such a major job to replace them, other needed rebuilding projects are usually included, pushing the cost up to $1000 to $2000. However, when it's completed, you may have a piano equal in tone to an upright costing $9000 or a grand worth $15000.

So you see, Pam, the owner has to decide whether the piano is worth spending that much money on it. A qualified piano rebuilder will help tremendously. He has the experience to know whether such an expenditure will produce an excellent result in this specific piano or whether it would be wiser to trade it for a new one. And he'll be glad to share his expertise.

Doctor Piano

Dear Doctor Piano,

When the tuner was here recently, I forgot to tell him that the pedal squeaks and I guess he didn't notice it. It's such an aggravation. Should I oil it myself?

Gladys M.

Dear Gladys,

No! Please don't! Oil can cause unbelievable damage to a piano if you get it in the wrong place. Anyway, most of the time, the squeak is caused by a problem quite a long way from the pedals.

I know it seems crazy – it sounds like it should be such a simple thing to correct, yet I've spent many frustrating minutes trying to find the source of an annoying squeak.

There I am, the wise and experienced piano technician – doing battle with a simple squeak. I look at six most common trouble spots, tighten screws or use special lubricants and I think I've got it. I put the piano back together again and invite the owner to try it out. Suddenly she stops playing, fixes me with a look of disdain (usually reserved for the puppy who soils the carpet) and says, "It still squeaks."

If it seems to take your favorite tuner a long time to fix a squeak, be sympathetic. Offer him a cup of coffee. It might go a long way in easing his frustration and restoring his faith in pianos.

Simple squeaks usually aren't.

Doctor Piano

Dear Doctor Piano,

There are a couple of notes on my piano that make a buzzing noise when I play them. What's wrong?

Charles H.

Dear Charles,

You've just described one of the most difficult and frustrating problems in piano maintenance. Don't be surprised if the technician asks for your help. It takes two people to find a buzz, one to pound the offending key and the other to examine and touch problem areas in and around the piano which might be causing the noise.(The tuner usually mutters unprintable things under his breath.) Does anybody know if they have psychics who can find such things?

Buzzes can be caused by extremely simple things that are easy to correct or by extremely serious problems which are expensive or even impossible to solve.

The other day, Charles, after trying a number of things to find the cause of a buzz and coming up empty, I looked in the back of the piano. There it was – a golf ball resting against the soundboard.

A lamp on top of the piano may cause a buzz or even a picture on the wall. Or perhaps a part inside the piano needs tightening. Tricky things to find but easy to fix.

Another common source of buzzes is a loose soundboard. Easy to find but expensive to fix. The most economical repair is to re-glue the soundboard to the ribs ($50 to $100) The best way, but only for very valuable instruments, is to have the piano rebuilt ($1000 to $2000)

I hope you never have a buzz in your piano, Charles. But, if you do, call your favorite tuner. Help him all you can and pay him for his frustration.

Doctor Piano

Dear Doctor Piano,

My piano has been giving trouble lately. Some of the notes don't stay in tune. When you press one key, it sounds like you've played two notes. My tuner says the pins are loose. What does that mean?

Merlette S.

Dear Merlette,

If you look inside your piano, you'll see rows and rows of steel pins and you'll notice that there's a wire wrapped around each of them. These are the tuning pins and they're about 2 inches long. They go through the steel plate into a hard, wooden "pin block". When the piano is new, these pins fit so tightly that they won't slip even though each string pulls with about 165 pounds of tension.

However, if the pinblock wasn't properly made or if the piano has been subjected to extremes of damp and dry climatic conditions, the wood may shrink and fail to grip the pins tightly enough. Then they'll slip, allowing the strings to go out of tune immediately. The piano is useless unless the condition is corrected.

If the loose pins seem to be a result of persistent dry air in the home, installing a climate control system may restore their tightness enough to make the piano useable again.(See the section on THE WEATHER AND YOUR PIANO for more information on this system)

Fortunately, Merlette, if this fails, the problem can be solved in several other ways. If the piano is very valuable, a new pinblock may be installed. However, with the related rebuilding, the cost may be several thousand dollars. Or, if the pinblock is sound, it may be sufficient to replace the original pins with oversized ones, at a cost of $600 to $800. This usually restores the life of the piano amazingly. If the piano is on its last legs, a liquid treatment may provide the solution. The cost is about $150 with tuning and it usually makes the piano playable again.

So you see, Merlette, it's a scary thing to be told that you have loose pins but it's not necessarily the end of the road.

Doctor Piano

Dear Doctor Piano,

Maybe I'm more suspicious than I should be. But, when somebody tells me I need to buy something, I like to check it out to see if he's putting one over on me. My piano tuner says our piano needs "voicing." What's that? Do I really need it?

Bev C.

Dear Bev,

I don't blame you. Glad I can help.

Let's start at the beginning. The sound of the piano is produced when the strings are struck by hammers made of compressed felt tightly stretched over a wooden moulding. When the hammers are new, they have just the right balance of firmness and resilience to produce tones that are clear but not harsh, mellow yet resonant.

As time goes by, the hammers tend to change. Long practicing gradually hardens them and cuts them. Climatic conditions cause them to become harder still and the tone of the piano becomes something it was never intended to be. "Voicing" is the tuner's term for restoring the hammer's shape and its proper degree of firmness.

You may need it, Bev. If your piano sounds shrill or harsh or strident, it may be that the hammers need to be voiced. The cost will be from $50 to $200. However, there may be other maladjustments in the action which are helping to cause the poor tone, so the bill can go higher.

The whole operation of "Regulating the tone" requires a very high level of skill, experience and sensitivity and not all tuners are equipped to do a good job.

So, Bev, if you think your piano's voice sounds a little sick, call your favorite tuner and show him the patient. He may recommend voicing or action regulating or something else. But trust him; when he gets finished, your piano will sing with a brand new beauty.

Doctor Piano

Dear Doctor Piano,

The keys on our piano are all chipped. What happened and how do I get them fixed?

Ben D.

Dear Ben,

Little children cause the problem. They wander around the house in search of things to touch, twist or bang. There sit those gleaming white keys about eye level—like the siren to the sailors: irresistible. They can't help themselves. They just have to find a stick or toy to pound them with and there go the chips.

Fixing them isn't nearly so simple. The best repair is to have all the white key coverings replaced. The cost is about $350 and you won't be able to use the piano for a week or so. The coverings won't be made of ivory, but you'll have your choice of white or simulated ivory.

If only a few are chipped, your favorite tuner can replace them in your home. With care, he'll be able to make them look pretty good, but it's almost impossible to match the color exactly. And, it won't come cheap. There's a lot of work involved. Or, of course, Ben, you could just keep on using the piano as it is.

I'm not sure what to tell you to avoid the problem of chipped keys. It would be too restrictive to keep the lid down all the time. You want the children to touch the keys and explore the sounds of the piano. I guess you'll have to keep sticks out of their hands and try to teach them not to bang things.

Good luck, Ben.

Doctor Piano

Dear Doctor Piano,

I heard someone tell of a piano with a "broken plate". I didn't hear all the details but it didn't sound good. What is a broken plate?

Irene S.

Dear Irene,

Believe me—you don't want to know!

But if you're sitting in the house in the quiet of an evening and the piano suddenly goes, *"Bang!"* and several notes sound funny, you're about to learn.

It's the kind of thing that—if you've got one, Irene, your piano is totalled—a dead loss.

The "plate" is the steel back in a piano which withstands the pressure of the strings—about 20 tons. Occasionally, one will give way, probably because of a defect in the casting process. Then, because the rigidity is gone from the piano, it won't stay in tune.

This breakage is so rare that most tuners see only one or two in a lifetime—proof that if it happens it's due to an inherent weakness, not tuner error.

Ordinary welding won't fix a cracked plate—it simply cracks again beside the weld. If the piano is a good quality grand or an extremely valuable upright, there is a possibility that the plate can be taken out of the piano and welded by cast iron specialists. Since this is almost equal to rebuilding the piano, the cost will be very high. Still, it might be worth it.

However, I've heard of other kinds of repairs which might work. So, if you've got a piano with a broken plate, call your favorite tuner in case there's any chance that something can be done for it.

But you'd also better start looking for another piano; I don't hold out much hope for the broken one.

Doctor Piano

Dear Doctor Piano,

I know that nothing lasts forever. Even the best built of buildings or tools eventually wear out. Do pianos ever wear out?

Pearl M.

Dear Pearl,

A good piano is a very tough piece of equipment. It can stand up to an enormous amount of use (and abuse) for many years. A few things it can't stand: children pounding the keys with hard objects, water spilled into it, extremes of heat and cold, moisture and dryness; these are a piano's arch enemies.

Under normal use, a good piano will last a couple of lifetimes. But eventually, wear will show up. The hammers will become flattened from hitting the strings and must be reshaped or replaced. Felt parts under the keys wear thin and must be renewed. Tiny felt bushings which form the "hinges" for moving parts become loose and allow the hammers to flop sideways. These also must be replaced, a very time-consuming job. The strings themselves become crystallized and lose their rich sound. Other felt and leather parts in the action may wear out and have to be repaired.

Much of the time, the piano is not worth the cost of rebuilding. It takes a lot of work and money to make much difference in sound. Often, you're better off to trade for a new instrument.

But, if the piano is a high quality instrument and very valuable for musical or sentimental reasons, it may be worthwhile to undertake rebuilding. This may be partial, simply replacing the worst of the worn out parts (cost: a few hundred dollars) or it may be total, stripping down the piano completely and rebuilding almost everything (cost: $2000 to $4000 or more.)

Piano rebuilding is an exacting job, requiring special equipment and extremely careful, knowledgeable workmanship. Not all piano tuners attempt it. Don't allow anyone to start on your piano unless he's recommended by your favorite piano tuner. However, done right, the results can be very satisfying and almost all the original beauty may be returned to your piano for many more years.

Doctor Piano

Dear Doctor Piano,

Does a piano ever come to the end of its life? I'd hate to think of such a thing after having my grandmother's piano in my home for so many years. But I guess it could happen. Does a piano ever have to be thrown out?

Robert W.

Dear Robert,

Yes, it happens. I once had to tell a family, "Sorry, this piano can't be tuned. You've lost your $700."

They'd noticed a used piano advertised in the newspaper. It was a tidy, small size, just right for their apartment. And the wood was beautiful! It sounded bad, but it could be tuned (or so they thought).

Eagerly, they bought it. Then they called me, but it was too late! The pinblock had been damaged by a move to a dry climate and would no longer hold the tuning pins tight. The piano wasn't worth repairing. It needed to be thrown out!

Like a car, a piano should be disposed of when the cost of major repairs exceeds the value it would have when repaired. However, sometimes another person will buy it just as a "klunker" or for spare parts. But to sell that old thing to someone else as a worthwhile instrument would be dishonest.

I never heard what became of that piano. Maybe their child had to try to practice on it, horrible-sounding though it was. Or maybe they advertised it for sale in the newspaper. Did you go to see it? I hope you didn't buy it!

There are some good used pianos for sale, but there are some booby-traps, too. And usually, the average person can't tell the difference. To protect yourself, call your favorite piano tuner and have him check out the piano for you. Give him $35 for his time and expertise. It's money well spent. He may save you $700.

Doctor Piano

The Weather and Your Piano...

Dear Doctor Piano,

We spent quite a bit to buy a really fine piano for our children. Now, we're anxious to look after it properly and protect it from harm. What's the most dangerous threat to long life for a piano?

Hugh L.

Dear Hugh,

The greatest enemy of pianos is: DRY AIR. Or, to be more specific: Continual changes from damp air to dry air and back again. This really upsets and harms pianos.

But, do you realize it?—this is what happens in your home every year! In the summer, the moist air comes in through the open doors and windows. (The humidity soars to 60% or 70%.) Then, in the winter, you close up the house and let the furnace dry the air out. It may drop as low as 10% or 15% relative humidity. As your piano responds to these changes, the pitch rises or falls, the tuning deteriorates and, in severe cases, cracks may appear in the soundboard or the tuning pins may become loose.

What's the answer? Get a humidity gauge and work for a more even humidity in your home all year round. A good power humidifier on your furnace will bring up the percentage in the winter. (Check it frequently to make sure it's not plugged up.)

In the summer, keep the piano away from open windows and doors. If your house gets very damp, purchase a dehumidifier (ask your plumber).

If you're a perfectionist, talk to your piano tuner about a piano climate control system. It's a bit pricey (about $300) and requires filling with water every two or three weeks, but it really does the trick.

So, Hugh, now that you know how to do it, save your piano from its worst enemy: fluctuating humidity.

Doctor Piano

Dear Doctor Piano,

I've heard you name "seasonal humidity changes" as the factor that puts my piano out of tune. Could you explain what happens in a full year?

Marilyn J.

Dear Marilyn,

Certainly. I'll go through the year and describe the humidity changes in the Canadian Prairie region and how your piano responds.

Let's say that you have your piano tuned in October. The tuner raised the pitch slightly to bring it to the standard of A440 and it sounds beautiful. The furnace has been running for a few weeks and the relative humidity in the house is around 40%

Through November and December, nothing much changes and your piano keeps on sounding beautiful until Christmas.

Then, in January or February, we have a cold spell. The temperature goes down to -20 degrees Celsius. The furnace runs a lot more and, even though it is equipped with a good humidifier, to prevent damage to the house, the humidifier must be set back, temporarily, to 25% or 30%. This extra dryness causes the soundboard to flatten and the pitch to drop 10% to 15% of a half note. In the process, some of the beauty and purity of the tuning slips away and the tone becomes harsh. (Without the humidifier, the humidity might dip to 10%, causing your piano to sound quite "sour".)

If a "chinook" (warm wind) comes along and stays for several days, melting the snow, the humidity may shoot up again and some of the beauty may return to your piano.

With moderating weather in March and April, the humidity will move back up to 40%, your piano's pitch will return to A440 and it'll sound much better.

During May through August, the humidity will vary rather widely from 45% to 65%.(l0% to 15% less if your home has central air conditioning) Your piano's soundboard absorbs some of this extra moisture and pushes the pitch of the strings up 10% to 15% of a half note. The pitch will now be about A444 and your piano will begin to sound kind of "ringy". The tone will sound more mellow, but some notes will "vibrate" when they are played.

Rains and muggy weather may push the humidity up to 75%, making it a very unstable time for your piano. If you have a keen ear, you may be able to hear it change from one day to the next as it struggles to keep up with changing conditions.

In September, the furnace starts working again, the humidity goes back down to 40%, and your piano's pitch returns to A440. It sounds better than it did in July, but not as perfect as it did last October. Some of the beauty is back, but some will never return until the tuner comes again.

This yearly cycle of damp and dry conditions is not only hard on your piano's tuning but also causes stress to its structure. Loose tuning pins may result or even a cracked soundboard. Any measures you can adopt to reduce winter's dryness or summer's dampness will make the beauty of its tones and tuning last much longer. And – it may prevent structural damage as well.

Doctor Piano

Dear Doctor Piano,

We use our piano quite a lot, mostly for hymns and classical music, and we want it to sound as pure and harmonious as possible all the time. When is the best time of year to have it tuned?

Randy B.

Dear Randy,

Piano tuners aren't going to like me if I tell you this. They need to tune pianos all year round in order to make a living.

But—here goes: It's true. There are some times in the year which are better for tuning your piano and some are poorer.

Take July, for instance. It's a bad time to have your piano tuned. Summer heat waves and summer rains play havoc with the humidity and tend to throw pianos out of tune quickly. Nobody's practicing, anyway. Music lessons are taking a break. Maybe we all should take a break. Parents, pupils, teachers, piano tuners—let's all take a break in July.

August is a different matter. Even though houses may still contain some summer humidity, we need to get those pianos ready for the resumption of piano lessons and practicing.

September, October and November are busy months for pianos. Suddenly pupils, parents and teachers hear horrible sounds coming from their pianos and they ring for the piano tuner.

December is a good time to tune the piano. Pianists are coming home from college and it's time to sing Christmas carols! So, make sure the piano is harmonious.

January and February are the draggy months of the year. In spite of this, it's a good time to have pianos tuned. The humidity should remain relatively stable and pianos should stay beautifully in tune for months.

March through June is the time when most piano recitals, festivals and concerts take place. It's a very important time to be sure the piano sounds great.

To pinpoint the very best time of the year, we need to be aware that changes in humidity affect the piano's tuning stability. A rule of thumb is: *Tune one month after the furnace starts or stops working.*

If you call the tuner once a year, October is the best month. If twice: April and October. If three times, make it: April, September and December. If four times: May, September, November and March would be ideal.

It's up to you, Randy. It all depends on how perfect you want your piano to sound.

Doctor Piano

Dear Doctor Piano,

We have recently moved to the city. We brought our piano and we want to take care of it in the right way. Is it true that a piano should be tuned after it is moved? If so, how long should we wait before calling the tuner?

Jocelyn Van B.

Dear Jocelyn,

You've asked two excellent questions which show your understanding of a piano's needs.

Yes, a piano should be tuned after it's moved, unless it's just within the same room. Often, the vibration of moving will cause changes in the tuning. As well, a move downstairs or to another building will place it in a different humidity environment and this'll cause it to go out of tune.

How long should you wait before the tuning? If the move is within the same city, two weeks or so will give the piano time enough to adjust to the new humidity and allow it to become stable again so that it'll hold a tuning well.

But if the move is between two cities of greatly different climates, say Vancouver and Calgary, for instance, or Toronto and Regina, the problem is much greater. The piano may take up to two years to completely adjust to the change and stabilize again.

However, to wait that long before tuning it will only aggravate the problem and cause additional damage to the piano. During the period of adjustment, having it checked and tuned frequently, is the best way to help it become stable again and avoid the huge pitch changes which often cause damage.

As you can realize, extra expense is involved, but I guess that's part of the cost of making such a move. You might inquire to see if your company or the furniture movers will cover the cost of this extra servicing.

I hope this helps, Jocelyn.

Doctor Piano

Dear Doctor Piano,

We are planning to move from Vancouver, British Columbia, a very damp climate, to Calgary, Alberta, where it's very dry. Will the move hurt our piano? How can we protect it from damage?

Lois S.

Dear Lois,

You're right to be concerned about the effect of climatic change on a piano. Moving between regions of damp and dry humidity is really hard on a piano.

In fact, if a piano has been built in a damp climate like England, bringing it to a dry prairie region like Alberta may deal it a mortal blow. The pitch will drop, moving parts will become loose, the hammers will harden, tuning pins will slip and the soundboard will split. To prevent this damage, some piano manufacturers build certain models specifically for extremely dry conditions.

You can help protect against damage to the piano by boosting the humidity in your home during the dry part of the year. But you must do it in a controlled way. Uncontrolled sources of moisture like unvented clothes dryers, hot tubs and indoor swimming pools will cause wild fluctuations in humidity. Your piano will sound wild, too.

Keeping the furnace thermostat a few degrees cooler in winter will help to avoid excessive dryness. Good for your piano and your heating bills, too.

A high quality, well-maintained furnace humidifier is one of the best answers to dryness. Set the humidistat around 40%, but be prepared to lower it during severe cold spells or condensation will run down your windows. Room type humidifiers are also helpful as long as they have a moisture control and as long as they're never allowed to run dry.

Moving from a dry climate to a damp one is much less traumatic for a piano. The tuning will be affected and the action may become sluggish, but usually, no worse damage occurs.

In both cases, a climate control system installed inside your piano will do the most to protect it from both extremes of humidity. These are available from piano tuners and piano stores and are well worth the money if you own a valuable piano.

Sometimes, however, a piano should be left behind when you move to a different climate. Have your favorite tuner look at your piano and discuss the situation with you.

Doctor Piano

Dear Doctor Piano,

Our piano is very old and in the cold weather it goes out of tune quickly. My mother said that a tuner once told her to put a jar of water in the bottom of the piano. Is this a good idea?

Jean S.

Dear Jean,

Not very. It doesn't do much good. The idea is all right–it's always a good thing to try to stabilize the moisture content of the air in and around a piano. In cold weather, when the furnace or fireplace is busy heating and drying out the air, any efforts to put moisture back in are worthwhile–a good power humidifier on the furnace, a room humidifier, etc.

However, Jean, a jar of water in the piano doesn't add enough moisture to make a difference. If, instead, you used a larger water container, and put a heating element above which would draw the water up through cloth wicks evaporating it into the air inside the piano, you'd have something. But then, you'd need an electronic control to turn off the humidifier when the proper degree of moisture is reached. Finally, to really do it right, the electronic control should have a de-humidifier in the piano which it can turn on to reduce excessive humidity in the damp season.

This all adds up to a climate control system which is already available through piano tuners and piano stores. It's a terrific system–the answer for pianos that go out of tune because of extreme changes in humidity. It's perfect for pianos in halls, churches, apartments and commercial buildings. But because most homes achieve a fairly reasonable balance in moisture conditions, such a system isn't really necessary unless there's a critical need that the piano stay precisely in tune all year round.

But you need to be aware, Jean, that if this system isn't properly installed and maintained, it can actually do harm to your piano. In such a case, your new piano warranty might be rendered void. And moving the piano without emptying the system could cause water spillage and damage.

Call your favorite tuner and ask him if he would recommend a climate control system for your particular situation. A bit pricey, about $300, but it may be the solution you've been looking for.(It'll save you more than that in damage protection and reduced tuning costs).

Doctor Piano

Dear Doctor Piano,

I play the piano at our church and Maribelle plays the organ. However, I notice that at certain times of the year they don't match in pitch. Why won't they stay in tune with each other?

Ethel H.

Dear Ethel,

It's the piano's fault. Pianos in churches and halls have a really tough time. The best solution is to have an organ that allows you to raise and lower the pitch to stay in tune with the piano.

Let me explain what happens. As you know, Ethel, the moist air of summer swells the piano's soundboard, causing it to go sharp in pitch and the dry air of winter shrinks it and makes it go flat.

What you may not know is that churches, halls and apartment blocks in the winter are like deserts. The furnace dries out the air and there's no source of moisture to replenish it. No humidifiers, no boiling kettles, no dishwashers, no one taking showers—dry as a desert. Winter and summer in such a situation cause a piano to vary widely in pitch and sometimes—cracks occur in the soundboard.

There's another solution: a piano climate control system. Installed inside an upright piano or underneath a covered grand piano, it keeps the humidity at 42% all year round. *Excellent!* Though it costs about $300 installed, every church and hall piano should have one. One caution, though: when the warning light starts blinking, the water container must be refilled (about every two to four weeks) or else the piano will go out of tune fairly quickly.

We must have heavenly harmony in churches. Maybe your church board should hear about it.

Doctor Piano

Dear Doctor Piano,

We bought a piano and we're trying to decide where to put it in the house. I heard a warning and I don't know if it's for real or an old wives' tale: "Never put a piano against an outside wall or in a basement." Is this true?

Dan C.

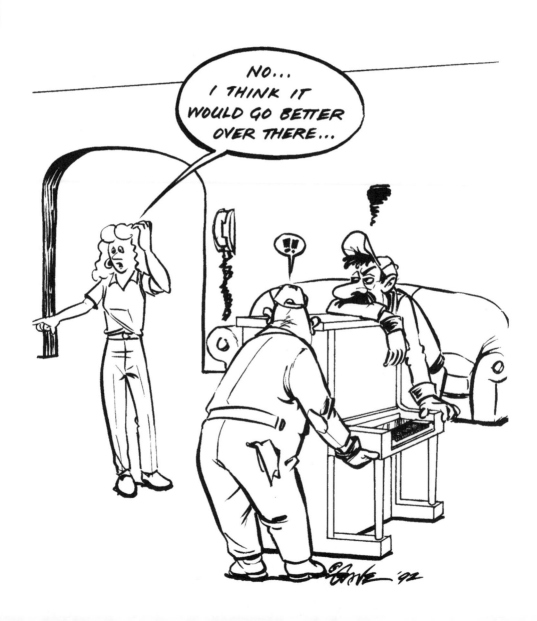

Dear Dan,

There are two issues here. Let me take them one at a time.

Placing a piano on an outside wall: Back in the old days, before houses had good insulation in the walls, this was an important piece of advice. In the winter, cold walls would collect moist air and pour it down into the piano, causing it to go out of tune – and worse. Then, the cold metal parts and strings would attract condensation and rust. Today, you don't need to avoid insulated outside walls unless they feel really cold in the winter.

But let me add something else. Whether it's the "Good Old Days" or the "Bad New Days", you must never place a piano over a hot air register or beside a hot radiator, stove or fireplace. The reason is similar – heat dries out the air and, if it pours into your piano, it'll put it out of tune and do other expensive damage. Direct sunlight or hot spotlights will do the same.

As for placing your piano in the basement, Dan, I think it's okay, provided it's in a pleasant environment for the musical life of your family.

What you want, for your piano's sake, is a place in your home where the temperature and humidity vary as little as possible. Especially in a dry climate, the lower level may be the best, since the air probably doesn't get quite as dry in the winter.

Of course, if you have flooding or obvious signs of dampness in your basement – IXNAY! Get your piano as far away from it as you can.

Dan, I hope this throws some light on the subject.

Doctor Piano

The Piano Tuner...

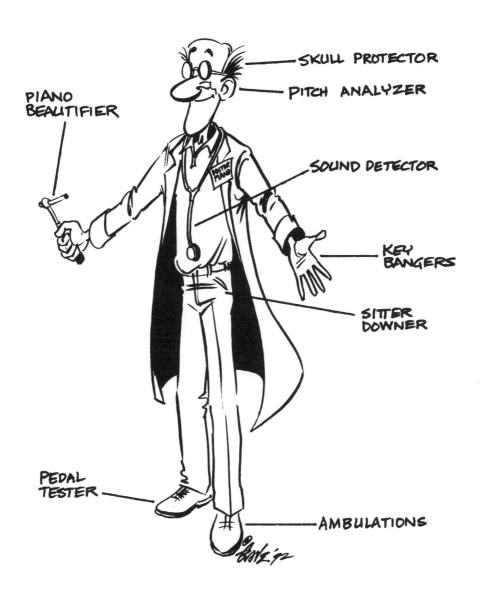

Dear Doctor Piano,

We've got to get our piano tuned but I don't know any tuners. I'm afraid, too, that I might get a bad one. Where can I find a good piano tuner?

David H.

Dear David,

It surprises me that you should ask that question, and yet, I've often heard people say they don't know how to find a piano technician. On the other side, there are lots of piano tuners spending big bucks on advertising so that people will know how to find them. Something isn't working right.

Perhaps I can help the situation. To find a piano tuner, look in the yellow pages of your telephone book. It'll surprise you to see how many men and women are ready and waiting to service your piano. "But", you feel like asking, "Are all these people as well qualified as they seem?"

I'm sure that most of them would do an adequate job on your piano, David, but if you want a specific recommendation, ask a piano teacher. She has usually found a satisfactory tuner and will be glad to recommend that person to you.

Other people to ask are: the manager of a concert hall, the owner of a piano store, the choir director of your church, a night club owner, your school music director, etc.

If you see the initials "RTT", "RPT", "PTG", or "CAPT" by a name, this is a worthwhile recommendation. It means that the tuner has passed examinations set by an organization of piano technicians – proof that he has a good basic knowledge of the craft.

Of course, the person who's in the best position to give you expert advice on finding a good tuner – is another piano tuner. He knows very well which ones are top technicians and which aren't. But, of course, if you ask him, you know what'll happen – he'll recommend himself! Naturally. Everyone believes in his own ability.

So, try the other sources I've suggested, David. Then, if you're still in doubt, give me a call and I'll recommend a real humdinger!

Doctor Piano

Dear Doctor Piano,

I was looking for a piano tuner in the yellow pages and I couldn't believe it! There are so many of them! Of course, I don't know one from the other. Does it matter who tunes my piano?

Dave G.

Dear Dave,

Yes, it does. Tuning a piano isn't like getting a haircut where, if you get a bad one, it'll grow out in a few days.

An inexperienced, untrained piano tuner can do life-long damage to your piano. He may break strings while tuning or overstretch them so that they lose their elasticity. He may bend tuning pins and they have to be replaced. Amateur efforts to regulate the tone may destroy the hammers. Other attempts to repair the action may cause deterioration of performance. Also, he'll be unaware of some of the regulation needs of the piano—thus they'll go uncorrected.

Perhaps the most consistent problem of inexperienced piano tuners is that they haven't yet learned how to set the tuning pins correctly while tuning. As a result, the pianos they service never stay properly in tune longer than a day or two.

That tuner may charge you less, but even then, you're probably not getting your money's worth.

Looking for a good tuner is like looking for a good dentist—you don't know what they're doing in there, so you'd better get the best known, the busiest, the most reputable technician you can find.

And, when you've found him—hang on to him!

Doctor Piano

Dear Doctor Piano,

The tuner serviced our piano the other day but I don't know how it's supposed to sound. How can I tell if the piano tuner did a good job on our piano?

Ed H.

Dear Ed,

It's not easy. A new dentist once looked in my mouth and said, "Hmmm. There's some good work in here and there's some bad work." Chills ran down my back and I resolved to stay away from any dentist who might be responsible for the "bad work."

It's not easy to tell good and bad tuning work, because the piano tuner is listening to sounds which the average person hasn't learned to distinguish.

Maybe a few guidelines will help, Ed:

1. Like picking a new dentist, find the tuner who is best recommended by music people you know.

2. Notice if he's disciplined and businesslike in his contact with you (this attitude will probably be reflected in the tuning job, also.)

3. When he's finished tuning, try playing a familiar piece on the piano (or get the tuner to do it.) It should sound great: clean and pure and harmonious. If the sound of the piano isn't beautiful to you, there's something wrong. It's like the man who asked his wife if his white shirt was clean enough to wear a second day. She said, "If it's doubtful, it's dirty!"

If the piano doesn't sound really good to you (provided it's a good quality piano) ask the tuner why. Perhaps other restorative work is needed. If you don't get a satisfactory answer, thank him, pay him and call someone else next time.

Doctor Piano

Dear Doctor Piano,

It seems that when some tuners tune a piano, it stays in tune better than when tuned by others. Is this true? Does the tuner have something to do with how long my piano stays in tune?

Grant N.

Dear Grant,

Yes, he does. There's a very delicate art in piano tuning called, "Setting The Pin". What it means is that when the tuner is adjusting the pitch of a piano string, he must turn the tuning pin so that the original bend and torsion of the pin are restored. If he fails to do this, he's leaving the pin in an unstable condition. With subsequent playing on the piano, the tuning pin will seek stability by bending or twisting itself and, in the process, the note will shift out of tune.

The same kind of thing happens with the wire string. It must be stretched and relaxed in such a way that it will not shift as the piano is used later.

The tuner who succeeds in these two operations will leave tunings that are solid – not altered by use of the piano, even vigorous use. If he doesn't, players of the piano will find that it'll go slightly out of tune almost immediately. Piano tuners know that they must succeed and that these skills are gained only after many years of experience.

There are many other influences that'll put your piano out of tune much quicker than the work of an inexperienced tuner. Loose pins will do it in a hurry. Humidity changes will put it drastically awry. But yes, Grant, you're right: the tuner has something to do with it.

Doctor Piano

Dear Doctor Piano,

The piano man was at our house yesterday, working on the piano. When the children made some noise, he would look at them and frown. Why does he want us to be so quiet when he's tuning our piano?

Keith and Donna E.

Dear Keith and Donna,

I know it's a pain. The problem is that he's listening to sounds which are very quiet and easy to overpower.

It may not seem like it, the way he pounds on the piano and the loud sounds he makes. But, it's the truth. He's not listening to the loud sounds which are splitting your eardrums. He's ignoring them and listening to the soft beats which determine the in-tuneness of the piano.

To hear them, he needs the house to be fairly quiet. Some noises are worse than others: rattling newspapers, music playing, clattering dishes, yelling kids. Sounds like these really make it hard for him and may result in a tuning job that's less than perfect.

Your tuner has learned to tolerate some background noise. Soft conversation in an adjoining room or a TV turned down very low shouldn't bother him. I heard of a tuner who made people stop their ticking clocks, but he was an exception.

So, my friends, if your favorite tuner asks for more quietness, be patient and try to help him. He's only human. The quieter and friendlier the home, the more effort he'll feel like putting into the task of making your piano sound like a string of pearls.

If not, who knows what may happen?

Doctor Piano

Dear Doctor Piano,

I hope this isn't too personal a question to ask you, but I've been wondering about it. I know you tune and service pianos. Do you play the piano?

Al J.

Dear Al,

This seems like an unusual question to ask a piano tuner but it's one that I hear very frequently. It's usually expressed: "I suppose you play the piano very well, don't you?" The implication is that a person would have to be a pianist in order to be able to tune a piano.

However Al, this isn't true. Piano tuning is a totally different art from performing piano music. A pianist and a piano tuner are listening to two different kinds of sounds and concentrating on two separate skills. The pianist is listening to the pitch and tone of the musical note. The piano tuner listens to the interference and re-enforcement of two piano strings when sounded together, placing them in proper relationship or unifying their sound.

Both of these persons have different goals. The pianist takes a musical selection and interprets it by touch, tone and timing until its melodies and harmonies strike some of the deepest emotional chords within us. His performance is a work of art.

For the piano tuner, his work of art is a piano prepared for performance. Its touch is eager and responsive. Its tone contains the potential for expressing the softness of evening breezes or the crashing thunder of summer storms. Each note rings true, adding richness to every subtle harmony. The piano shines and glows, like a string of pearls.

Both are important. But, because the piano tuner's approach to his work is so different from the pianist's, the ability to play the piano doesn't help him very much.

However, like the piano salesman who can't play the piano either, the piano tuner doesn't want you to think he's inadequate for his work because he's not a musical performer. So, he learns a little tune and a few chords to play for you. Or he does like a tuner friend of mine who, when asked if he plays the piano, always replies (with a smile), "I play at it all day long!"

Doctor Piano

Dear Doctor Piano,

We recently bought a piano and had it tuned and I was thinking about the tuner. He'll be coming to service the piano every six months for years to come. What do I have a right to expect from him?

Ellen B.

Dear Ellen,

That's an excellent question. You're going to be paying him $120 - $150 a year. You need to know what you should get for your money. Here's what I think:

1. Prompt, efficient, friendly service. And, he should keep his appointments faithfully or phone you about changes.

2. His tunings should bring out the beauty of your piano. They should last for several months (provided the piano and home conditions make this possible).

3. At each tuning, he should be able to give you an evaluation of the efficiency of your piano's action and an estimate of the cost of corrective adjustments.

4. When carrying out repairs or adjustments, he should be able to keep the final bill within 10% of the estimate or provide a satisfactory explanation.

5. If the piano is under warranty, he should notify you of any problems and support your claims to the dealer involved.

6. He should be able to give you a general assessment of the piano's suitability for the level of music you're playing on it. He may recommend rebuilding or replacing it as greater musical demands are made.

7. He should be available so that you can phone him for advice concerning piano service or purchases of instruments.

This seems like a long list, doesn't it, Ellen? But, I felt you should be aware of the important elements of a good working relationship between you and your piano tuner.

But, please—there are some things you shouldn't expect from him. Don't ask him to comment on the work of other piano technicians. Don't ask him to evaluate piano teachers and don't expect him to make trips to your piano for free.

Doctor Piano

Dear Doctor Piano,

Years ago, the man we used to have tuning our piano was blind. In fact, I don't remember hearing about any that weren't. Aren't piano tuners always blind?

Dot S.

Dear Dot,

Not always. But some of the finest piano tuners we have in North America are visually impaired. In probably a hundred ways, this is a disadvantage. Travelling is a problem. Some kinds of piano adjustments and repairs are difficult. (They're tough enough for me and I have good eyes.)

However, blind technicians have devised special tools and techniques which enable them to do complete and satisfactory piano service.

But there's one area where blindness is an asset. People who lose one of their senses tend to concentrate more on the remaining ones and use them to better advantage. Not being able to see, blind tuners focus on what they hear–probably much better than the rest of us. As a result, they're able to do superlative tuning work.

Dot, if you call a visually impaired technician to tune your piano, you can be of help. Open the door for him only if it swings away from him. Clear everything off the piano (as you should do for any tuner). If you have to lead him through the house to the piano, let him take your elbow and he'll be just fine.

After that, leave him alone. When he's finished, you'll be thrilled with your piano's new beauty.

Doctor Piano

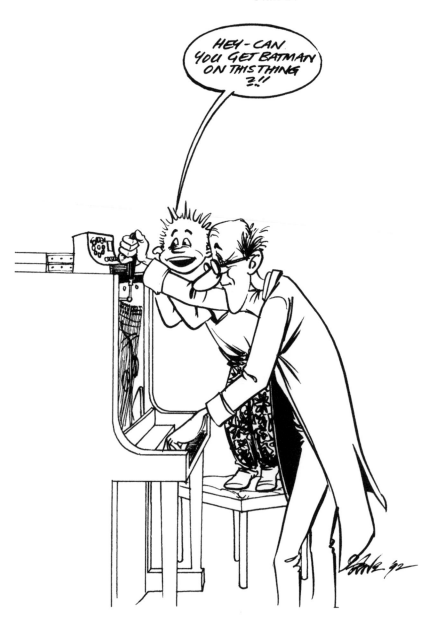

Dear Stan,

Maybe it was a television set and he was watching the World Series–no, I'm just joking.

That little box is an electronic tuning device which some tuners use to aid them in putting the piano in tune. But, as soon as I say that, you want to know if this is a better procedure than tuning the piano "by ear". No, it isn't.

The problem is: the electronic machine is perfect–accurate to 1/1000 of a half note. But pianos are not perfect. As a result, the tuner who uses one must calibrate the machine to make it fit the distortions and inaccuracies inherent in the average piano. Even when an electronic machine is used, the final stages of the process–tuning perfect unisons–still must be done by ear.

However, in the hands of an experienced tuner whose ears are well trained, the device can do a good job of tuning the piano. But, in the hands of a novice, who can't hear right and wrong sounds, it will sometimes produce terrible tunings.

So, Stan, it comes down to the same old story: A conscientious, experienced piano tuner will do a good job on your piano whether he uses an electronic device or not. In fact, many people believe that the tuner who doesn't use the device is the best choice.

In any case, when you find a piano tuner who makes your piano sound beautiful, hang on to him! Let him do a thorough job of maintaining your piano and keep him coming back every year or oftener.

Doctor Piano

Dear Doctor Piano,

I don't know if you remember, but you were at my house a few weeks ago. I noticed that while you were tuning the piano, every once in a while, you would reach in and pluck some strings with your fingernail. I didn't get a chance to ask you then. Why do you do that?

Bob H.

Dear Bob,

Thank you for being so observant. I like to have people watch, listen and ask questions while I'm tuning.

By plucking the strings, I wasn't trying to do an imitation of playing the harp. There's a better reason.

Most of the notes in a piano have two or three strings that must be tuned in unison to create the proper sound. When they are almost together, the sound isn't right. It may sound "wavy" or "sour" or "false". In piano tuning, "close" isn't good enough.

But for the tuner, striking the key to sound the group of three strings doesn't tell which string is wrong or whether it's above or below the proper pitch.

My solution is to pluck the three strings one after the other. In this way I can tell which string is off pitch: left, centre or right and whether it is above or below the others. It works well and helps me create a perfect unison of sound; but I never realized how odd it must sound to someone standing nearby.

And I'll tell you something else: it's hard on fingernails. The nail on the index finger of my right hand is broken down to the quick right now. I don't know what to do about that problem, Bob. Maybe you'd have the answer for me. I'd be glad to hear from you.

Doctor Piano

Dear Doctor Piano,

I was listening to the man tune our piano as you told us to. But every once in a while he would give the key an awful bang. It nearly took the top of my head off. Why does he do that?

Faye Y.

Dear Faye,

I'm sorry that happened; I guess that's one of the hazards of staying in the room with the piano tuner. But keep on doing it. Ask him to demonstrate what to listen for and keep on listening.

I'll tell you a secret—those loud bangs hurt his ears, too. But there's an important reason for doing it. Important enough that even though he doesn't like it, he must keep on making those terrible loud sounds.

Here's why: A piano string passes over several friction points from the bottom of the piano up to the tuning pin. When the tuner tightens the string by turning the tuning pin, the string sometimes gets partially stuck at one of these points. One way to get it loose is to give the key a loud bang. So, he does it.

There are other ways of getting the string unstuck, but they are tricky to accomplish. The point is, however, no matter what method he chooses, the tuner must succeed in getting each string to move properly. If he fails, the piano won't stay in tune.

This is no small task, especially when you consider that there are usually about 230 strings in the average piano.

Most people that I tune for, marvel that I have to do so much work in tuning their piano. But that's all right, I'm trained to do it and I enjoy it. It's far better than making your kids practice on a terrible sounding piano.

Doctor Piano

Dear Doctor Piano,

I don't know what I should pay for piano tuning and I feel vulnerable. The piano tuner spent 2 hours at my house and charged me $75.00. Isn't that a bit too much?

Helen C.

Dear Helen,

You're the very first person to ask me this question, but I'm sure lots of other people have thought it.

The implication is that piano tuners must be getting rich. Let me tell you something: they're not. They make an average living like most other people.

Three factors make the fees seem high. First, the piano tuner spends a lot of time and money travelling from house to house (I drive 60 or more kilometres every day and spend about two hours of my working time doing it.)

Second, there are seasons of the year when the piano tuner is prevented from working. From the middle of June to the middle of August, many people are thinking more about their vacations than their pianos. Christmas, New Year and Easter are the same. In fact, every long weekend means two or three days of lost income for the tuner.

Third, because he's self-employed, the tuner loses out on employer-paid benefits like days off, vacations with pay, pension plans, etc. And nobody pays him when he's sick. To make up for these things, he has to charge a bit more for his work.

All of this seems reasonable, but it doesn't make you feel any better, does it, Helen? Cheer up. If the plumber comes to your house and works for two hours, he'll charge you more than that.

Of course, you can always hunt around for a cheaper plumber—if you want to take the chance.

Doctor Piano

Dear Doctor Piano,

Yesterday, the piano tuner worked on my piano. Because it had been several years since it was tuned, he had to raise the pitch and added that charge to the regular fee. It made a big bill! Then, he said that it had to be tuned again in 6 weeks! Is it going to cost as much next time?

Cheryl H.

Dear Cheryl,

I'm sorry that happened. It's not nice to face sudden unexpected costs when you're trying to maintain the family piano.

The problem was that regular tunings had been neglected for some years. As a result, the pitch had dropped so much that a once-over tuning to the correct pitch was impossible. So, a pitch-raising operation had to be performed first—at an extra cost of $15 to $30, making a total cost of $80 to $95.

The worst result was that even with a careful pitch raise and a fine tuning, the piano will not stay properly in tune at this time. It must be tuned again in six or eight weeks.

I don't blame you for asking about the cost of the next visit, Cheryl. However, you need to realize that another pitch raise will not be necessary if the piano is tuned again within a proper length of time. That'll save you $15 to $30. Then, perhaps your tuner will give you a discount for having the piano tuned within one year or less—another saving.

Even so, neglect has cost you $75 to $80 more than you expected. Naturally, you don't feel very happy about that. Look at it this way: the extra cost has just made up for what you didn't spend during the time when the piano was being neglected.

But from now on, I hope you'll make sure to have your piano tuned regularly and avoid the big tuning bill.

Doctor Piano

Dear Doctor Piano,

A string broke while the man was tuning my piano last week and then he charged me $20 for a new one. I didn't feel very good about that but I paid him. Was he fair with me?

Dorothy H.

Dear Dorothy,

Maybe or maybe not. It's hard to tell.

But, Dorothy, let me tell you something. The mechanic broke a bolt when he was repairing your car the other day. He had to drill out the broken piece, re-thread the hole and put in a new bolt. You may not have heard about it but you paid for it. Was that fair?

The point is that both the bolt and the piano string were probably old, crystallized and weak and the mechanic or the tuner should not be blamed because they broke. It's one of the unavoidable hazards of repair work. Weakened parts may break even though the technician is as careful as he can be.

It's possible though, Dorothy, that the string was broken through the tuner's carelessness. He accidentally put his tuning lever on the wrong pin and when he turned it too far, the string snapped.

Now what? If he's conscientious, he'll probably replace the string without cost to you. Most craftsmen take pride in their skill and in the finished product they produce. They're not interested in charging the customer for their mistakes.

Make sure you find such a piano tuner, one whose ethics and expertise you can trust. Then, relax. He'll be fair with you.

Doctor Piano

Dear Doctor Piano,

I can hear some out-of-tune notes in my piano. Would it be possible for me to buy a tuning lever and fix them myself?

Lee R.

Dear Lee,

Yes, of course. If you own a rather poor piano which has some strings that slip out of tune quickly, this might be a temporary way to resolve painful discords. But I have to give you some warnings:

1. It's easy to make a mistake and break a string.

2. The notes you correct will go out of tune more quickly than ever.

3. You may leave the piano worse than you found it, even though some notes sound smoother.

4. You may spend a lot of time tinkering with the piano and still be unsatisfied.

However, Lee, before you try it, ask your favorite tuner about it. Be prepared to have him discourage you, though. He may feel that you might do more harm than good. If you can't persuade him, you'd better give up the idea, for without his help, you will definitely create more problems than you'll solve.

On the other hand, if you're a person with a good quality piano, this do-it-yourself idea isn't for you. A good piano goes out of tune in such a subtle, widespread way that the only proper treatment is a thorough tuning job by a professional.

Lee, I hope I've given you enough information that you can make a good decision.

Doctor Piano

Dear Doctor Piano,

I hope you won't mind my taking up your time, Doctor, since I am not one of your clients. I am also a professional piano technician. This question has been plaguing me and I'm sure you've probably asked the same question yourself. Why doesn't anybody ever bother to thank the piano tuner?

Otto K.

Dear Otto,

No problem. Thanks for asking it. I understand your question because I feel that way, too.

I know – my pay should be thanks enough. But I do it for more than pay. I tune pianos to create beauty. I tune pianos to give a beautiful instrument to the people I work for.

Oh, it's true – some people say, "Thanks", as I go out the door. But that's not what I mean.

Sometimes I take extra pains to make the piano especially perfect and I voice the hammers a bit to give the tone that special mellow glow. I can just imagine the pianist in the family coming home, sitting down and running his fingers over the keys. "Mmmm", he says, "This is beautiful. I'm going to phone that tuner and tell him how much I like it." But, he never does it.

They never do. Maybe they play half the night because the beauty of a freshly tuned piano draws the music out like magic. But they never phone me and let me know.

Sometimes, I even ask for it. I say to the parents, "When Judy (Grade 10 piano pupil) comes home, have her call me and tell me how she likes it." They say they will but they never do.

Judy came home all right and I'm sure she must have loved the piano because I did my best work on it, but she never phoned.

Like the Maytag repairman – piano tuners have feelings, too.

Doctor Piano